M-MAT
Multi-Modal
Attachment Therapy

Also Available

Understanding Attachment Injuries in Children and
How to Help: A Guide for Parents and Caregivers

by *Catherine A Young*

Visit the website: www.m-mat.org *for more information*

M-MAT
Multi-Modal
Attachment Therapy

An Integrated Whole-Brain
Approach to Attachment Injuries
in Children and Families

Expanded Second Edition

CATHERINE A. YOUNG

Granite Swan Press
Groveland, CA

ISBN 978-1-7335703-4-3
ISBN 978-1-7335703-5-0 (ebook)

Library of Congress Control Number: 2021935738

All examples and dialogue in this book are constructed from over 25 years of experience and do not represent any single individual or set of individuals. All names are entirely fictitious. Any similarity to real persons, living or dead, is coincidental and not intended by the author.

Excerpt from article, "Bonding and Attachment in Maltreated Children," by Bruce Perry, MD, Ph.D. (childtrauma.org).
Reprinted by permission.

Published by Granite Swan Press
P.O. Box 122
Groveland CA 95321

Visit www.m-mat.org

Visit www.graniteswanpress.com

Visit www.facebook.com/MultiModalAttachmentTherapy

This book is dedicated to all of the creative and caring therapists who walk with children and families on their healing journeys, and the courageous children and families who allow us to walk with them. I have been privileged to know a few!

Contents

Therapeutic Stance
Structure
Course of Therapy

5 M-MAT Play: The Frame Part 1

What is Attachment-Based Play and Why?
Fun and Play in Attachment
Elements of M-MAT Play
Guidelines for Implementing M-MAT Play
What To Do When...

6 M-MAT Feeding and Questions: The Frame Part 2

What are Feeding and Attachment Questions and Why?
Attachment Questions
Process

7 M-MAT Talk

What is M-MAT talk and Why?
Re-Storying
Skill Building
Psychoeducation
Addressing Behavior
Integrating other Modalities/Therapeutic Tools
Conclusion

8 Working with Parents

Getting the Parents on Board
Attachment-Based Parenting
Parent Support
Homework
Working with Biological Parents vs
Other Caregivers
Conclusion

Acknowledgements

It takes the courage of people putting their ideas on paper throughout the years to allow therapies to develop and evolve. I wish to acknowledge all those who have done so, and so have, in their own way, contributed to this work. These include, among others, Carl Rogers with his discussions of unconditional positive regard, empathy, and authenticity, which still set the foundation for many therapies today; Mary Ainsworth and John Bowlby, who brought the concept of attachment to the fore; Cloe Madanes with her work with families impacted by abuse; and Daniel Hughes, Ph.D., Bruce Perry, MD, Ph.D., and Daniel Siegel, MD, whose more recent works bring contemporary ideas to the treatment of children and families.

I would further like to acknowledge the architects of Narrative Therapy, Theraplay®, and Cognitive Behavioral Therapy, whose contributions are evident in my work.

I've come to know these therapies and individuals through trainings and writings, and I am grateful to all. I've attempted to give credit, where due, throughout the book.

Finally, I would like to acknowledge Lisa, Jennifer and Martin for their unerring editorial acumen, and Whitney, Amber and Ben for their input and support.

Introduction

Children struggling with attachment injuries are often sad, angry, anxious, depressed, hurting and hurtful to others but do not respond well to traditional child therapies. These children have been deeply injured in the first few years of their lives in their primary relationship; the relationship that is supposed to support, protect and nurture their young selves. They are struggling, and yet they often reject the very things they need for healing: love, relationship and connection. This presents unique challenges for both parents and therapists.

Perhaps there is a better way to reach these children. Perhaps our therapy models have simply not been a good match for the needs of children with attachment injuries.

I have worked as a therapist with children with severe emotional/behavioral concerns, and their families, for over twenty-five years. I have further supported other therapists in their work with children and families in my role as a clinical supervisor. One of my first clinical jobs was in a public mental health day treatment program for children 7 to 12 years of age. Many of these children were one step away from being removed from their homes due to their behavioral/emotional difficulties. Up to that point, the training I had received and the reading I had done in child therapy had been primarily in non-directive play therapy and behavior therapy. I soon found that these children needed something much more. They needed more structure, more relationship focus, and more direction to help them move out of destructive patterns and cycles.

I went in search of more effective therapies. I learned EFT (Emotional Freedom Technique) and EMDR (Eye Movement Desensitization and Reprocessing) which I often found helpful in reducing trauma symptoms in children. I was also excited to discover Narrative Therapy which provided a useful framework and interventions for helping children re-story their lives. When I discovered attachment therapies, I began to see hope for developing a consistently effective and efficient therapy to help these children and create the kind of pervasive, second-order change I was looking for.

I studied, read books, and attended seminars and workshops in attachment therapy. The earliest targeted attachment therapies that I am aware of included the controversial holding therapy, and other practices, that led many to be concerned. Early attachment therapies seemed to go to an extreme in being directive and controlling. Perhaps this was in response to the frustration and futility of utilizing non-directive therapies in addressing attachment injuries in children; or to these children's own frequent, highly controlling behaviors.

I was then exposed to therapists like Daniel Hughes, Ph.D., and Daniel Siegel, MD, who had much gentler approaches with positive results. I further attended a two-day workshop on Theraplay® and was introduced to the concept of attachment-based play.

I developed my own version of attachment-based play using the components I felt were most critical to supporting attachment. Once I combined this attachment-based play with an attachment-focused, narrative, cognitive behavioral talk portion, I began to see more lasting, transformational changes in the children I worked with. I was further able to observe the same kinds of positive changes in the clients of the therapists I was able to coach in this model.

I have taken elements of various therapy modalities (attachment-based play, other attachment-based therapies, cognitive behavioral therapy, narrative therapy, play therapy, solution-focused therapy and, I am sure, other therapy models that I have absorbed over the years) and brought them together in a new, organized and systematic therapy model that I have found very effective in reaching these very challenging children.

Because it needs a name, I call this model Multi-Modal Attachment Therapy (M-MAT). I call it Multi-Modal Attachment Therapy simply because it integrates a variety of therapeutic modalities in a systematic way to treat children with significant attachment injuries.

M-MAT is specifically designed to meet the needs of attachment-injured children. In a whole-brain approach, M-MAT blends several modalities to target precisely those areas most impacted by the attachment injury: attachment, self-image, worldview, and skills deficits. The result is a powerful, cohesive, and comprehensive attachment-based therapy.

I have watched children transform from detached, angry, aggressive, emotionally disorganized, sometimes bizarre, sometimes withdrawn beings into loving, happy, emotionally connected children. These children have historically been so challenging to treat that I have had parents tell me that other professionals told them not to expect too much of their child; not to expect too much love, too much growth, too much connection from these injured children.

I have had adoptive parents come to me as a last resort. Though very much committed to their child, they do not know if they can continue to have their child in their home. They are losing hope. They have tried everything, including therapy, sometimes for years, to no avail. For the child, the loss of a loving home, the thing they most need for healing, is a tragedy with lasting, devastating effects for both the child and society at large. It is this that has motivated me to write this book with the wish to rekindle hope for these families, healing for these children, and efficacy for the therapists working to help them.

1

Orientation to this Book

Purpose

This book is a practical manual for therapists in implementing Multi-Modal Attachment Therapy (M-MAT). It may also hold some use for parents and other professionals in understanding attachment and approaches to working with children with attachment injuries.

Scope and Limitations of this Book

In order to identify the therapy needs of attachment-injured children, and thus understand the underpinnings of the M-MAT model, this book includes a brief overview of attachment theory and a discussion of children who struggle with attachment injuries. This is not an exhaustive discussion of attachment theory, as that is beyond the scope of this book, and there are many good resources that cover this information. Even if one has studied attachment theory extensively, however, it will be useful to read these sections as the perspectives expressed in this book specifically inform this therapy model.

The bulk of this book is devoted to understanding the principles and practice of Multi-Modal Attachment Therapy (M-MAT). M-MAT is primarily designed for children 5 to 12 years of age with mild to severe attachment injuries who have at least one adult in their life who is both committed to them and able to participate in the therapy. Teens can also be treated with M-MAT, with some adjustment, as discussed in chapter 9.

One group that poses special challenges, is most at-risk and most likely to fall through the cracks, is the subset of children who do not have an adult committed to them and/ or able to participate in therapy. This can include foster children in temporary placements, children whose parents are absent or deceased, or children whose parents or caregivers have addiction issues or mental health issues that interfere with their ability to care for their child and/or participate in treatment. It may include an adoptive parent who is no longer committed to their adopted child or a long-term guardian who is unwilling to participate in the therapy, perhaps due to their own attachment injuries.

These children can be helped with Multi-Modal Attachment Therapy Individual (M-MAT Individual), which is discussed in chapter 10 of this book. The M-MAT model is the foundational model, and understanding the principles and procedures of this model is fundamental to understanding how to work individually with attachment-injured children. The M-MAT Individual model is an adaptation of the M-MAT model.

Terms

Throughout this book, the terms "caregiver" and "parent" will be used interchangeably to mean the child's primary caregiver(s), whether that is a relative, foster or adoptive parent, biological parent, or guardian. For ease of writing and reading, the terms parent and caregiver can mean either one or two caregivers.

In the examples, "Mom" will be used in dialogue to represent the primary caregiver, but it could as easily be Dad, Auntie, Grandma, etc., as appropriate.

The term "therapist" will also be used in the broadest sense possible, to include counselors, clinical social workers, psychologists and others who provide therapy to children.

I will also use the term attachment injury rather than attachment disorder. Children with attachment injuries have a range of attachment difficulties, from mild to severe, with a variety of presentations. I like the term attachment injury because it separates the child from the injury, and injuries can heal. Like the physical metaphor, some injuries require intervention to heal or heal well. Furthermore, the term "Reactive Attachment Disorder" is narrowly defined in the *Diagnostic and Statistical Manual of Mental Disorders, Fifth Edition* (DSM-5) and has developed many emotionally charged associations over the years. "Disinhibited Social Engagement Disorder" (new to the DSM-5 and previously "Reactive Attachment Disorder, disinhibited type" in DSM-IV) is likewise limited, describing only one presentation of the attachment-injured child.

I occasionally use the term "attachment-injured child" to indicate a child with moderate to severe untreated attachment injuries. This is for ease of communication and not an attempt to label children. All children are more than their struggles, including children struggling with attachment injuries. Like any child, a child with attachment injuries may be bright, or musical, or creative, or have a good sense of humor, or display any other number of strengths that are a part of the whole person.

For brevity's sake, Multi-Modal Attachment Therapy will often be referred to as M-MAT.

For ease of reading, singular they, and its derivatives (their, them), will be used as needed for gender-neutral pronouns, consistent with spoken language and evolving written language norms, and in lieu of the more awkward "he or she" and derivatives.

Hopes for this Book

My primary hope for this book is that the many talented, committed and creative therapists in the world are able to implement the principles and practices outlined in this book to facilitate healing for children and families.

My second hope is that researchers will be able to conduct rigorous studies to validate this model. I can only speak to my experiences as a therapist and clinical supervisor as to the validity of this model, and, in this age of evidence-based practices, research has become critical for the use of effective practices in many settings. M-MAT's highly structured nature lends itself to study and replication, and it, therefore, is a good candidate for research.

2

Attachment Theory Overview

Attachment theory postulates that the attachment, or connection, that a child forms with their primary caregiver during the first three years of life has a dramatic and profound effect on that child's development. Emotional, behavioral, moral, and relational aspects of the child's life are greatly impacted by their first relationships.

Attachment is defined by Bruce Perry, MD, Ph.D., as an enduring emotional relationship with a specific person that brings safety, comfort, soothing and pleasure, and the loss or threatened loss of the person brings intense distress. Further, the child finds comfort and safety in the context of this relationship. Note that the relationship is enduring and emotional and that it is with a specific person. For the infant to develop an appropriate attachment, there needs to be at least one specific, consistent person in their life that provides safety, soothing, comfort and pleasure. The first, or primary, attachment is usually between infant and mother and sets the template for all future attachments.

Attachment is related to brain development. Bruce Perry, MD, Ph.D., succinctly ties attachment to early brain development in this passage from "Bonding and Attachment in Maltreated Children" (www.childtrauma.org):

The capacity and desire to form emotional relationships is related to the organization and functioning of specific parts of the human brain. Just as the brain allows us to see, smell, taste, think, talk and move, it is the organ that allows us to love -- or not. The systems in the human brain that allow us to form and maintain emotional relationships develop during infancy and the first years of life. Experiences during this early vulnerable period of life are critical to shaping the capacity to form intimate and emotionally healthy relationships.

Thus, we can view attachment injuries as the underdevelopment of portions of the brain. This is useful when we think of treatment and how to exercise and stimulate the brain in order to increase the capacity for healthy attachment.

It is important to note that a child's brain is still young and still has a great capacity to grow and change based on the input it receives. The term neuroplasticity refers to the ability of the brain to change and grow based on experiences. Neuroplasticity occurs throughout the lifespan, but never more so than in childhood.

While trauma can impact the brain, healing can as well. When we have experiences, those experiences cause neurons to fire. Repeated experiences strengthen neural pathways and more strongly affect the brain and nervous system. This underlines the importance of repetition and consistency in healing.

Attachment refers not only to infant-parent relationships but to relationships with close friends, family and partners as well. It is the first relationships, however, that set the stage for the child's subsequent relationships. The quality and nature of a person's later attachments, or their ability to attach at all, is strongly dependent on their first, primary attachment.

Attachment is not something the child does or the parent does. Rather, it is the connection that is developed through the reciprocal interaction between parent and child. When the child cries, the parent responds. When the parent makes silly noises, the child smiles. Ideally, the parent is attuned to their child's signals, providing stimulation, comfort, and affection. Through positive interactions with their caregiver, the child forms a sense of self-worth, a sense of efficacy in the world, and a template for all future relationships.

A child's healthy attachment to their caregiver is instrumental in helping the child develop a positive sense of self, the ability to regulate emotion, a strong moral compass, resiliency in the face of challenges, prosocial behavior and empathy towards others. Resiliency research indicates that even just one healthy attachment/relationship in a child's life has a strong impact on the child's resilience and well-being over time.

A child sustains attachment injury when their attachment to their primary caregiver has been significantly disrupted in the first few years of life. When untreated, the child may face issues of low self-esteem, difficulty regulating emotions, and lack of empathy towards others. They may display disruptive, anti-social or even bizarre behaviors. Though these children may be bright, they will often struggle to cope with the challenges of life, and their ability to establish healthy relationships will be severely impaired. Anxiety, anger and depression are common. Those trying to parent these children often feel like failures as nothing seems to work. Many adoptive and foster family placements fail due to unaddressed attachment injuries. Attachment injuries can equally be a concern for children in their biological homes when there has been early disrupted attachment.

Many things can disrupt a child's attachment, including both caregiver factors and child factors.

Caregiver factors include:

- Multiple, sequential caregivers - A child can benefit from multiple caregivers if these are co-occurring and consistent over time, as in an extended family. If multiple caregivers are sequential, however, such as a child moving from foster home to foster home, significant damage can be done as each caregiver attachment is broken, one after the other. By definition, foster and adopted children have suffered attachment injury, having lost at least one primary attachment. The more they move around from home to home, the greater the potential for injury.

- Impairment in the caregiver's ability to respond appropriately to the child - This may include anything from depression, illness, substance abuse, mental illness, domestic violence, prolonged separation, or a parent with their own attachment injuries impairing their ability to respond to their child.

- Parental abuse and neglect - Severe neglect can be even more damaging than abuse to a child's attachment. The child who is not responded to at all can be more injured in their attachment than the child who is responded to harshly. Perhaps one of the most challenging parenting patterns for a child to cope with is severe neglect with unpredictable, sporadic abuse.

- Custody issues may contribute to attachment difficulties - For instance, attachment injury can occur when the child moves from a more stable parent's home to a less stable parent's home. The child experiences abandonment by the relatively healthy parent to whatever dangers exist in the home of the unstable parent, thus impairing their attachment to both.

Child factors include:

- Anything that may impair a child's ability to respond to their caregiver, including the child's illness, chronic pain, disability, or extended separation from their caregiver.

Although different children will respond differently, generally speaking, the more severe and pervasive the disruption, the higher the potential for harm. Not all children experiencing the above will have significant attachment injuries. There are protective factors such as other significant relationships, child temperament, and subsequent care, to name a few, that play a role in health and injury as well.

In addition to individual costs of attachment injuries, there are also societal costs. Social service, health, and law enforcement costs can be related to attachment-injured individuals. If left untreated, attachment injury is passed from generation to generation along with cycles of abuse and neglect. For every child who heals from attachment injury, there is benefit to the child, the family, and society at large.

For the purposes of M-MAT, children with attachment difficulties will be defined as children with attachment injuries. The term attachment injury is broader and more inclusive than attachment disorder and suggests a continuum of severity from mild to severe, and, like all injuries, there is an implied potential for healing.

3

Children with Attachment Injuries

Understanding Attachment Injuries in Children

When presenting on attachment theory and therapy, I only half-jokingly state that we all have attachment issues. Certainly, many people have early relational challenges with their parents. This is what can make even adult relationships so difficult. Most people, however, are able to work out their early relational issues throughout their lives and subsequent relationships, sometimes with the help of therapy. When the attachment injury is too severe, however, the child rejects the love and support they need for healing. One way to conceptualize an attachment injury is as an anxiety disorder. The child becomes so anxious and phobic about relationships (while at the same time desperately needing healthy relationship) that they push away, in every way possible, from those who might help.

The first three years of a child's life are crucial in the development of appropriate attachments. Severe disruptions during this period can be very damaging. It can be difficult for caregivers to understand why the child is having such difficulties when they are now in a loving, supportive home. The problem is that the child holds in their body and mind the experience that relationships are hurtful, painful, and life threatening and, additionally, that there is something wrong with them. Furthermore, from a neuroscience perspective, the parts of the brain involved in healthy attachment are likely underdeveloped, so the capacity for connection is impaired.

Take the example of a child who, for the first six months of life, lived in a situation where the parent suffered from addiction and mental health disabilities. This parent was passed out when their child was crying for food or comfort. When awake, the parent was highly irritable and screamed at the baby when they fussed too much. The child was malnourished and underweight. Maybe the parent had a partner that was abusive to them.

Perhaps at six months, the baby is removed from the home due to severe neglect. The child is preverbal, but what they have already learned is that they have no power to control their environment (lack of responsiveness to their cries), and while there is a biological imperative for the infant to be close to the caregiver for survival, the infant has found that the caregiver has threatened their survival and is unsafe. It is unsafe to try and get needs met, but also unsafe not to. The infant has learned that the big people in their life are to be feared and avoided. In the new home, the baby may be very quiet, avoidant, fussy, or alternately clingy and avoidant.

The new parents receiving this beautiful baby into their home may have no idea of the child's injury and the potential impact on the child's life, much less how to best support healing for the child. Fortunately, the child is young, their brain is still very young, and if the parents are knowledgeable and skilled, there is a chance for healing. If not, the child may be set up for lifelong difficulties.

Imagine, further, that this child stayed in their biological home until they were three years old. Maybe the parent was sometimes OK, but most of the time wasn't. The child now has a schema for parent and relationship that includes unpredictable, dangerous, hurtful and unhelpful. The child has learned that it is up to their 3-year-old self to get even their most basic needs met. The child cannot count on anyone. Tied to these ideas is the belief, because young children are naturally egocentric, that it is their fault. Something is fundamentally wrong with them for their parent to behave this way. The child is NOT OK, NOT lovable. There is no joy in this child's life. The brain develops to 90% of its adult size by age three. In this case, this amazing brain development has largely centered on survival and creating this cognitive schema in order to understand and cope in the world.

Children with attachment injuries tend to have the following beliefs:

• Adults, at best, have nothing to offer emotionally and, at worst, are deeply hurtful.
• Relationships are unsafe, scary and anxiety provoking.
• The child is unloveable/bad.
• There is no one upon whom the child can depend.

As a result, the child feels deeply alone, ungrounded, empty and anxious, but does not know what they are missing.

Although the child may not be consciously aware of them, these core beliefs about themselves, relationships and caregivers are very rigid and do not change easily. They generate self-defeating, destructive behavior that perpetuates the faulty beliefs and pushes away the very support they so desperately need. This behavior can include:

- **Easily dysregulated/difficulty calming** - This can include long temper tantrums and rages that can be highly disruptive to family functioning. Parents may report that they feel they need to walk on eggshells around their child. Difficulty in regulating emotions may stem from the lack of parental soothing and co-regulation when younger. Young children learn to regulate their emotions with support from their parents or primary caregivers. When they have not had that early parental support, they may not have the skills or brain development necessary for self-regulation.

- **Rejects adult efforts to help them regulate** - This can be very frustrating to parents trying to help their child, particularly when their efforts seem to make things worse.

- **Will not seek out caregivers for comfort, sharing or support** - Sometimes this child may appear pseudo mature, with a high level of independence and little need for their caregiver.

- **Poor eye contact or eye contact on their terms only** - One of a young child's primary ways of communicating and receiving information from their caregivers is through eye contact. In a healthy parent/infant interaction, the child will receive reassurance and validation from their parent through eye contact. Young children will also assess the safety of a situation with an eye contact check-in with their parents. In an unhealthy situation, when all the child has received through eye contact is anger and hurt, or eye contact has been absent altogether, they will stop engaging in this way.

- **Primitive/injurious self-soothing behaviors** - This may include behaviors such as scratching themselves when in high distress or head banging. An older child may revert to thumb sucking, rocking or other behaviors generally associated with younger children.

- **Controlling behaviors** - The child may seem to have a need to be in charge or control of every instance, often with frequent challenging of, or arguing with, adults. The child that has experienced parents who were either incapable of being in control or, when in control, were scary and unsafe has learned that to feel safe, they need to feel in control.

- **Fragile ego, poor winner/poor loser** - This child does not do well with competition. The core belief that they are not OK makes losing intolerable and winning something to brag about in an attempt to keep at bay their bad feelings about themselves. They may also be hypersensitive to any kind of criticism or negative feedback from both peers and adults for the same reason.

- **Poor impulse control** - The child may have difficulty thinking before acting, leading to difficulties in school, at home and with peers.

- **Hypervigilance** - The child is usually quite aware of what is happening around them, being extremely alert to any possible threat or danger. Their very survival may have depended on being able to read the cues in their environment and caregivers.

- **Aggression** - Kicking, hitting, scratching and biting are not unusual. The child may also exhibit aggression towards pets and animals. Aggression may be due to emotional dysregulation, poor impulse control, re-enactment of their own trauma, and/or expression of anger in unhealthy ways.

- **Splitting of adults** - The child may work at splitting the adults in their life as a matter of course. That may mean going to different adults to get different answers or trying to get one adult to side with them against another adult (most often the primary caregiver).

- **Eating issues/food hoarding** - This may be related to early food deprivation and/or be symbolic of the nurturing they so desperately need. It is not unusual for parents or caregivers to find food stuffed in nooks and crannies in the child's bedroom or for children to sneak out at night to raid the refrigerator or cabinets.

- **Can be superficially charming** - This strategy may have helped ensure the child's survival and allowed them to get at least some of their needs met. This can be particularly frustrating to parents when their child is charming with everyone else but angry, irritable and/or dismissive with them.

- **Indiscriminate/poor boundaries with unfamiliar adults** - The child may go to anyone. They may jump in a stranger's lap. The child is seeking safety in an unsafe manner, and, for the unaware adult, this behavior may seem endearing, but the connection does not go very deep. In this child's world, one adult is easily exchanged for another adult. There is no discrimination, no particular connection to one adult. This behavior also sets the child up to be further victimized.

- **Lack of empathy** - The child's belief in a hostile world and that, at the core, they are not OK, along with their own deep neediness, make it difficult for them to have empathy towards others.

- **Nonsense lying and storytelling** - Most children lie for a reason, either to get (e.g., a sweet) or avoid (e.g., punishment) something. The attachment-injured child may lie for no apparent reason. Parents may report that the child will insist that the sky is yellow or make up a story about something that happened at school that never actually happened with no apparent goal or reason. Sometimes they will tell very elaborate stories that are clearly not true. Sometimes these stories will have an ego protective or bolstering function, such as stories in which they beat up bad guys, or have accomplished unrealistic things, or have possessions they do not have.

- **Bizarre behaviors** - These can include anything well outside the range of normal. An example might be a child who offers their urine to peers as "lemonade".

- **Peer problems** - Attachment-injured children will often have one of three ways of being with peers: they may be easily victimized and picked on due to their low self-esteem; they may be the bully or aggressor, again due to their low self-esteem (and it may seem a good alternative to being a victim, as no one wants to be a victim); or they may not seem to care about their peer interactions at all due to their disconnect with people in general. Sometimes a child alternates between being a bully and a victim in their peer interactions. Sometimes children with attachment injuries will look to peers to meet their primary attachment needs. This is a strategy that is bound to fail as their peers are unable to provide them the nurturing, stability, limit setting and maturity that they need. They may present as a leader or follower in these situations.

- **Anxiety and depression** - Attachment-injured children can also be highly anxious and often suffer from depression.

Of course, not all attachment-injured children will have all of these behaviors, and each child is unique. Below are a few examples of how significant attachment injuries may manifest in children:

- 12-year-old is bright but is a bully and overeats. Child is big and hurts other children in sneaky ways, e.g., pushing and tripping, when no one is looking. Has no positive peer relationships. Appears to lack empathy. Attempts to control people and situations.
- 5-year-old has hour-long rages. Hits, kicks, throws things, screams. Scratches self, threatens to jump out of a window. Difficulty with both family and peer relations. Highly sensitive to perceived peer rejection.
- 11-year-old engages in nonsensical lying, baffling caregivers. Child has no peer connections, does not seem to want friends, and acts bizarrely with peers, e.g., offering dead bugs to eat like candy.
- 9-year-old attempts to push infant sibling out a second-story window. Avoids eye contact. Sneaks out of bedroom at night. Hoards food.
- 4-year-old is bright and makes everything a battle. Argues about everything. Refuses cooperation with even simple

tasks. Rages for extended periods. Is a master at engaging parents in nonsensical arguments.
- 13-year-old runs from home often. "Hates" parent. Gets in trouble with peers. Is very promiscuous with unsafe sexual behaviors. Easily emotionally dysregulated wherein screams and yells and runs. Has tried various drugs. Is fully out of parental control. Sees any attempt of parent to help as an attempt to hurt.
- 8-year-old seems cute and charming outside the home but regularly assaults parent in the home, hitting, kicking, and scratching, leaving bruises and marks.

The attachment-injured child is likely to display their most challenging behaviors with their primary caregiver, usually the mother. All the rage, anger and hurt is directed at the symbol of the person who was supposed to love them and be there for them unconditionally. Sometimes they appear to function well with others or in other settings so that people begin to question the mother or primary caregiver's competence. It is not at all unusual for the mother or primary caregiver to be blamed by others for the child's difficulties with the reasoning that the child, "Does not behave that way with me!"

Although the assessment of Reactive Attachment Disorder and attachment injuries is beyond the scope of the book, attachment injuries are often evident from the first meeting with parent and child. Some obvious signs that there are attachment issues afoot:

- The child comes into the room for the first time and never references the parent. The child never looks at or to the parent and never asks anything of the parent. The child may play with toys in the room but does not try in any way to engage the parent. This child may try to engage the therapist while ignoring the parent or may ignore the adults in the room altogether.

- The child is excessively familiar with the therapist physically and/or verbally, e.g., the child meets the therapist for the first time and tries to hug the therapist or jump on the therapist's lap, or says they love the therapist.
- The child displays excessively controlling behavior, trying to control the parent's behavior, the situation, the therapy and the therapist.

Worldview of Children with Attachment Injuries

To understand the child's behavior and why traditional therapies have so often failed children with attachment injuries, it is useful to go further into the worldview of the attachment-injured child.

To borrow a concept from Narrative Therapy, the attachment-injured child has organized their experiences into a story or narrative in which parents, at best, have nothing to offer and, at worst, are deeply hurtful. Even when now placed in a new environment with loving parents, the child sees only the facts and incidents that fit with the initial story or will bend and interpret facts to fit within that framework. The child holds a rigid and dysfunctional template for relationships.

In addition, when there has been severe neglect or an unstable, chaotic early environment, the child has not learned that what they do actually matters or makes a difference. The child has no sense of efficacy. The child does not develop a good understanding of cause and effect. Research confirms that children who experience early trauma have a deficit in their cause and effect reasoning.

Furthermore, the child feels deeply alone. There is no one upon whom the child can depend. This creates a great deal of anxiety. To ward off this anxiety, the child often tries to control the environment and, even more strongly, tries to control interactions with the primary caregiver. The high anxiety associated with relationship, and the rigidity of the child's relational template, cause the child to push away from the things they need most for healing, closeness and attachment, keeping the attachment-injured child in a state of disconnect.

Attachment-injured Children and Behavior

While parents would like their children to behave because it is the right thing to do, many children, and especially attachment-injured children, are not that advanced in their thinking or moral development. For children with attachment injuries, fear, anger, anxiety, hurt, and low self-worth all contribute to lashing out. Poor impulse control and poor self-regulation can be contributing factors as well. These children may also be re-enacting abuse they experienced or observed in their early years.

Attachment-injured children are often run by two opposing forces: the need to connect and the fear-driven need to keep emotional distance. Negative behavior is one way to connect with caregivers through the caregiver's emotional response to the behavior while at the same time maintaining or creating emotional distance. Sometimes the child's impulse to push away others can result in very hurtful behavior. It may be much more in keeping with the child's worldview to accept an angry response from a parent rather than a loving response. It merely confirms what they already think they know: they are bad, and their parents don't love them.

In the worldview of a child with attachment injuries, they are not OK, and the people around them are not OK. Therefore, there is little motivation to behave. Also, the child may gain a strong sense of power by acting out either aggressively or passive-aggressively, which further supports the problematic behavior. For attachment-injured children, this is a defense against the extreme powerlessness and fear they experienced when very young. It is not unusual to find that the whole household is run around the child's extreme behaviors. When that happens, it only feeds the maladaptive behavior.

Some of the most challenging behavior for parents to cope with may not be behavior that occurs during a temper tantrum (i.e., while the child is emotionally dysregulated) but rather, any apparently calculated, destructive, or hurtful behavior. For example, a child sneaking and breaking a parent's prize possession. To understand the behavior, we need only look at the consequences of the behavior. It likely pushes the parent away (creating emotional distance and, thus, a sense of safety) and angers the parent (creating a sense of power and control). The parent's response also establishes an emotional connection between child and parent, even if it is a negative one. So the behavior has served to create connection and a sense of power and control while simultaneously pushing away closeness.

It may also be the only way the child knows how to express anger or frustration. Perhaps the child is mad at their parent for setting a limit. They don't know how to say they are mad. They don't know how to express their frustration, and so they act out. The anger may be amplified by the many real hurts they experienced at the hands of caregivers when younger. At that moment, they may actually be acting from a past hurt, triggered by a perceived current slight. Sneaky and passive-aggressive behavior, in particular, can be an indication that a child does not feel safe expressing difficult emotions and/or does not know how.

Attachment-injured children also may have had no structure, limits, or boundaries in the earliest part of their lives. If so, they can be like untamed beings with the expectation of doing what they want when they want. Thus, they may perceive any parental boundaries or limits as the parent wanting to unfairly control them.

Attachment-injured children do not readily take responsibility for their behavior. Of course, many children avoid responsibility for wrongdoing to avoid getting in trouble or due to feelings of guilt or shame. The attachment-injured child, however, may take this to an extreme. This may include lying when the evidence of their wrongdoing is incontrovertible (while their hand is still in the proverbial cookie jar). They may stick to their lie no matter what, blaming others and throwing a tantrum when caught or questioned.

This is likely a defense against intolerable feelings of shame they may feel when caught and/or the fear of getting in trouble. It is also possible that getting in trouble, when the child was very little, led to physical and/or verbal abuse, which may have been life-threatening, or perceived by the child as life-threatening. This denial of responsibility, therefore, can be a survival strategy. Anything associated with survival is more strongly held in the brain and nervous system and will likely take longer to change than other behavior.

M-MAT aims to increase a child's tolerance and acceptance of positive attention and thus give them the space to move away from negative, attention-seeking behaviors.

The Failure of Traditional Therapies with Attachment-Injured Children

The dysfunctional relational template and impaired cause and effect reasoning of attachment-injured children are largely responsible for why they do not respond well to traditional behavioral interventions. In fact, behavioral interventions can make the child worse because the child will interpret consequences as another injustice done to them, consistent with the initial narrative of their lives, and positive reinforcers as an attempt to control them.

Positive reinforcers, often treats, desired objects or privileges, sometimes do not work at all because the child's perceived need for control far outweighs the reward. The child may view a behavior plan as an attempt to control them, and giving up control, in their body/mind schema, is dangerous. Other times the child may comply temporarily in order to obtain the reinforcer but then fall right back into previous behavior because the forces driving the behavior are still present.

For behavioral interventions to work, the child must believe, deep down, that the caregiver has their best interest at heart and must be able to connect their behavior to consequences and rewards in a cause and effect manner. If not, behavioral interventions become a game and a power struggle between child and caregiver. If the child cannot rebel directly, they may become sneaky and get back at the caregiver in sneaky or passive-aggressive ways.

For example, when a parent tries to give the child a time out in their room for behavior, the child may have little sense that they created the time out by their behavior. Rather, they believe the parent is being 'mean' and does not like them, which generates anger, hurt, and the continued belief that they are bad, further generating extreme and difficult behavior. If the parent uses a reward system, the child may feel that the parent is trying to control them. They may go along until they get the desired reward and then act out, or, if they do not earn the reward, they again may feel the parent is being mean to them. Alternately, the reward may have little meaning for them at all.

Their interpretations, of course, are consistent with the narrative through which they organize all of their experiences and information. Events inconsistent with the original narrative are either not noticed or misinterpreted. Thus, despite the parents' best efforts, the child gets worse over time rather than better.

A teenage youth may state, with genuine anger and hurt, that, when they were little, their parents removed all their toys from their room, only to share a moment later in the conversation that they routinely broke and threw their toys. Or, with the same deep hurt, relay that their parents took away all their privileges at a time when they were completely out of control, running the streets, doing drugs, lying, and disobeying all household rules. The hurt that they feel comes from their earliest sense of abandonment, fear and anger, the only lens through which they are able to view their later experiences. Therefore consequences, both natural and otherwise, feel like just another hurt that their parent or the world is inflicting upon them, strengthening an already negative worldview.

Another traditional child therapy is non-directive play therapy, a la Virginia Axline. In non-directive play therapy, the child is largely left to their own devices with minimal structure and direction from the therapist. The therapist provides reflective and mirroring responses. This can be an effective therapy for many children and many situations. For the attachment-injured child, however, this too closely mirrors their earliest experiences of neglect. The child is still alone. The child is still without limits and structure and an adult to help make sense of their world. The mirroring and reflective responses that the therapist provides are not harmful but are not enough to break through the initial narrative.

Sometimes, in non-directive play, the attachment-injured child will move away from open-ended imaginative play because it is too anxiety provoking. Sometimes the child will repeat a theme over and over again in a way that appears stuck. Other times, the child will be very controlling of the therapist in the play session, telling them what to do in every instance. And sometimes, the child will enact in play a high level of violence that is repetitive, feels counterproductive, and never seems to get resolved.

I have had many parents bring their children to me after months or even years of therapy that has not succeeded in bringing about any significant positive change. The child is injured in the area of relationship; it is through relationship that the child needs to be healed. Hands-off, non-directive play therapy is insufficient in these circumstances. If healing occurs in this context, it is most likely due to the therapeutic relationship, but this is a long, long road. It is possible that a mildly attachment-injured child with a non-directive play therapist could make some improvement over many years with the therapist, but then it likely would be primarily the safe, stable, long-term relationship that is providing the healing. Far more often, this therapy fails to address the child's needs altogether.

Cognitive Behavioral Therapy (CBT) and skills-based therapies (e.g., self-soothing skills, communication skills) are useful when integrated into a larger attachment-based therapy, as they are in M-MAT, but, by themselves, fall short with the attachment-injured child. This is because they only address the issue from a cognitive, verbal perspective. Much of attachment injury is preverbal and body oriented. We know young children need touch, eye contact, and play, all nonverbal avenues of growth, for appropriate development and attachment.

For skill-building based therapies, attachment-injured children often will not cooperate. If they do cooperate in the session and learn some skills, they often will not apply them in real-life situations. They hold the beliefs that their parent is trying to hurt them and that they are bad, and so they have no motivation to get their anger or behavior under control. Their anger and acting out may be the only sense of power and control they have in their lives, and they are unwilling to give that up. They need to both change their underlying beliefs and begin to experience a positive attachment before the skill building can be effective.

Yet another approach to treatment of these treatment-resistant children is medication. It is not unusual for attachment-injured children to be on any of a number of medications to help them to calm, to focus, and to reduce depression and anxiety and other symptoms. For some children, medication seems to be helpful in conjunction with therapy, and a psychiatric referral is often in order. For no attachment-injured child, however, is medication alone the answer. A relational injury requires a relational intervention. Of course, children's symptoms are often complex, and a thorough evaluation by a child psychiatrist can be very useful.

In summary, children with attachment injuries have traditionally been extremely difficult to treat due to their rigid core beliefs or worldview. Many traditional child therapies have their place and can be integrated into effective therapy, but only when attachment is put center stage in the therapy process, as it is in Multi-Modal Attachment Therapy (M-MAT).

Attachment Injuries and Mental Health Diagnoses

The young child with significantly disrupted attachment will often respond in one of two ways with others, either with inhibited attachment or disinhibited attachment. In the *Diagnostic and Statistical Manual of Mental Disorders, Fifth Edition* (DSM-5), these are accounted for in Reactive Attachment Disorder and Disinhibited Social Engagement Disorder, respectively.

Inhibited attachment: These children will act as if adults do not exist in their world. They have come to believe that adults have nothing to offer them. They do not come to adults for solace, safety or assistance. They do not look to adults for positive interactions of any kind. They have no positive expectations of adults. In their world, they have come to rely only on themselves.

Disinhibited attachment: These children will go to anyone at any time. They do not differentiate between the familiar and the stranger. They do not develop specific attachments to anyone. People are interchangeable. Although they can be charming, their relationships are superficial. They have learned to look everywhere and anywhere to try to get their physical and emotional needs met. They will often jump into the lap of a stranger or take the hand of someone they have never met, while at the same time being emotionally avoidant of their caregiver. They are vulnerable to being victimized due to their neediness and lack of discrimination and are easily led into trouble by others.

The DSM-5 descriptions of these diagnoses are rather narrow and do not capture the wide range of behaviors seen in children with severely injured attachment (such as nonsense lying or controlling behaviors). Furthermore, the DSM-5 diagnoses focus on children up to 5 years of age and caution is suggested in making these diagnoses after age 5. Therefore, latency age children are not well accounted for in these diagnoses.

For these reasons, the broader terms "attachment injury" and "attachment-injured child" are used throughout this book to refer to attachment disorders and children with significant attachment injuries.

Whether the child exhibits inhibited or disinhibited attachment patterns, their ability to form strong, positive, reciprocal relationships is severely impaired. Those trying to engage in a relationship with them will often feel manipulated because these children have not learned what it is to truly relate to another human being. Sadly, while these children may feel empty inside, they do not really know what they are missing.

There are a number of other mental health diagnoses commonly given to children with attachment injuries. Attachment-injured children often meet the DSM-5 criteria for Disruptive Mood Dysregulation Disorder, which is categorized as a depressive disorder. Eating, mood and anxiety disorders are also common, as are Oppositional Defiant Disorder and Conduct Disorder. Posttraumatic Stress Disorder (PTSD) may be present, either diagnosed or undiagnosed. Attention Deficit Hyperactivity Disorder (ADHD) is sometimes attributed to these children.

There was a period when many attachment-injured children were being diagnosed with the somewhat controversial Pediatric Bipolar Disorder. Subsequent research indicates that these children more likely suffered from a depressive disorder, which is now better captured in Disruptive Mood Dysregulation Disorder.

As children with attachment injuries get older, some may be identified with "borderline" or "narcissistic" or "antisocial" traits, and untreated attachment injuries may develop into personality disorders.

4

Multi-Modal Attachment Therapy (M-MAT) Overview

Multi-Modal Attachment Therapy (M-MAT) is a structured attachment-based therapy with the primary focus on healing attachment injuries through adult/child interactions, integrating both play and talk therapies.

Toward an Effective Attachment Therapy

Most therapies were not designed with attachment injuries in mind. There are four things that get in the way of the attachment-injured child progressing in both the therapy and their lives: lack of attachment, defensiveness against relationship, rigid relational templates, and a dysfunctional life story or narrative that leads to a negative self-image and view of the world. To be most effective, an attachment therapy needs to address all of these.

An effective therapy for attachment-injured children, then, requires interventions that reduce defensiveness while exercising and strengthening the neural pathways associated with attachment and relationship. It further needs to shift the child's relational template, helping them view love, family and relationship in a new light. Finally, it needs to support the child in re-storying their life in an adaptive, healthy way, allowing for a healthy self-image and worldview. A useful attachment therapy will also help the child build skills in areas that may have been impacted by trauma or attachment injury.

As you read through the following pages, consider how M-MAT accomplishes these objectives.

Target Population

M-MAT is designed for children 5 to 12 years of age struggling with mild to severe attachment injuries, along with at least one adult caregiver committed to the child. M-MAT has been successfully implemented outside this age range with children from 4 to 16 years of age. Adjusting for age and working with teens are discussed in chapter 9. An adaptation for working with children without a primary caregiver available can be found in Chapter 10.

The parent involved in the therapy needs to be the primary caregiver for the child. This might be an adoptive parent, long-term foster parent, guardian, relative caregiver (grandparent, aunt, uncle) or biological parent. Attachment and resiliency research tells us that even one strong positive attachment is protective. Once the child has developed a strong primary attachment, they will be in a better position to make positive connections with others. If there are two parents involved with the child, the work can be done with both parents, but it may be best to start with the primary caregiver and introduce the other parent further along in the therapy.

Unfortunately, not all children have a committed adult able to do this work. Fortunately, there is a variation of this model, M-MAT Individual, modified specifically for individual therapy with attachment-injured children. See chapter 10: M-MAT Individual.

Concepts

The following are key concepts of Multi-Modal Attachment Therapy (M-MAT). How these are implemented in the therapy will become clear in the following chapters.

1. The primary focus of healing in M-MAT is relational. The goal of the therapy is to heal the attachment/relational injuries so the child can then access all the resources that healthy attachment allows, both within themself and with others, in order to reach their full potential as a human being.

2. M-MAT is a two-pronged approach with both a play and a talk component. The play component utilizes largely non-verbal forms of communication, connection and nurturing, such as mirroring, rhythm, touch and eye contact. The talk component engages the power of language and the child's thoughts by addressing cognitive distortions, responsibility, and self-concept through re-storying, skill building and psychoeducation, creating a new narrative in which the child can organize and make sense of their experiences in a healthy, adaptive way.

    Together, the two components reinforce each other, allow for deeper integration and healing, and are far more powerful than either alone. Together they access many parts of the brain and harness the incredible healing power inherent in both left and right brain modalities. This is a whole-brain approach that uses both bottom-up (sensory and body-oriented) and top-down (cognitive) therapeutic interventions.

If we presume that the child with attachment injuries has parts of the brain that are underdeveloped, the parts associated with attachment and relationship, then the goal is to stimulate and develop these parts of the child's brain through experiences of play and talk. Both the play and talk components of M-MAT are described in detail in further chapters.

3. M-MAT's focus is on the relationship between the child and caregiver. The therapist takes every opportunity in session to redirect the child to the parent or caregiver. For instance, if a child asks the therapist a question that can be easily answered by the parent, the therapist will redirect the child to the parent. If the child is coming to the therapist for affection or nurturing, the therapist will redirect to the parent. If the therapist is working with a caregiver who is the child's mother or father, biological or adoptive, the therapist will address the parent in the parent/child session by "Mom" or "Dad" (or equivalent) to reinforce the parent's role in the child's life. The focus is on the parent/child relationship. The therapy not only helps the child feel connected to the parent, but helps the parent connect to the child as well. The healing is in the relationship for all parties involved.

4. M-MAT is a structured therapy. There is a lot of room for the therapist to be creative and to adjust the session to best meet the child's needs, but each session maintains a three part structure with a beginning (attachment-based

play), middle (talk), and end (questions and feeding). Each of these parts has its own purpose, but the structure, in and of itself, is also therapeutic and an important part of the intervention.

A consistent, predictable structure provides safety, supports emotional regulation, and reduces anxiety, allowing the child to process and participate more easily. Children with attachment injuries are often highly anxious and often feel a need to control their environment and those around them. A safe, predictable structure helps them relax and let go of that control.

The structure also provides a sense of ritual and corrects the unpredictability and lack of structure likely experienced in the child's earliest years. Once they are familiar with the structure, both parents and children often find it comforting.

5. M-MAT is a regressive therapy. That is to say, in the therapy session, the child is allowed to regress to a younger age. This is particularly true in the attachment-based play. Play activities are used that would often be associated with a younger child. The child's relational injuries occurred at a young age, and the purpose of the therapy is to go back to address those early injuries and practice the early interactions the child may have missed.

Keep in mind that children with significant attachment issues are already emotionally young, although they may appear pseudo-mature. Of course, the therapist can modify the activities and therapy based on the child's developmental age, needs and abilities.

Some people may worry that the child will come out of the session in a permanently regressed state. Simply put, that does not happen. Occasionally the child may temporarily seek out younger activities or forms of nurturing, or display younger behavior. The therapist can encourage the caregiver to fulfill the needs the child is expressing, within reason. More commonly, the child will allow themself to regress in the session, while outside the session, they will begin to display a higher level of maturity than they did previously. As the course of therapy progresses, the child will catch up to their chronological age, maturing in their ability to engage in the talk portion of the therapy in-session and to handle life stressors outside of session.

6. M-MAT takes a hierarchical approach. In the session, the adults are in charge. These children need SOMEONE to be in charge. They have been left to their own devices way too long and have developed pathology due to it. They are often extremely controlling in an effort to create predictability and safety for themselves. It is up to the adults to create that predictability and safety. The child needs to learn that the adults can be in charge, and it can be safe and even FUN! Often, if the therapist comes in unprepared to the session or unsure what to do, the child will sense the uncertainty and try to take charge. A sign of progress in the therapy is the child's willingness to let go of control.

7. Along the same lines, M-MAT is a directive therapy. The parent and child have likely been struggling for a long time, and it is not doing them a service to have them try to figure it out themselves. If they knew how to make things better, they would have done so already. The child is generally emotionally bankrupt and fearful of relationship, without the resources (knowledge or skills) to do anything different. The parents are often frustrated and exhausted. Their usual parenting skills have not worked. Parents can be quite relieved to have someone help them understand what is happening and teach them

skills to address it. That being said, it is always important to be sensitive to the parent's beliefs and to work with them collaboratively to achieve the best results. This is further explored in chapter 8: Working with Parents.

8. Attachment-based play is a fundamental component of M-MAT. Attachment-based play (discussed in chapter 5: M-MAT Play) provides the foundation for all of the other work in the therapy. It is a key in healing attachment injuries and also prepares and allows the child to do the other therapy work. Attachment-based play is likely the intervention that most directly stimulates the parts of the child's brain associated with early attachment development.

9. M-MAT endeavors to create a new story or narrative for the child that is adaptive and promotes emotional health. This concept is borrowed from Narrative Therapy. The dominant or maladaptive story that organizes the child's perceptions and filters their experiences usually includes such concepts as: I'm not loved or lovable; there is something wrong with me and/or the adults around me; I am all alone; bad things have happened because I'm bad; to get close is to get hurt, etc. M-MAT creates an alternative story in which the child recognizes that they are loved and lovable, and where relationships become a source of comfort and joy rather than fear and pain. In M-MAT, this is accomplished through both cognitive and experiential processes, including a re-telling of the child's life story (the attachment narrative) addressing key issues and misperceptions; noticing and focusing on evidence, current and past, that supports the new story; and creating new, alternate relational experiences both in and outside the therapy.

10. M-MAT is always respectful of the child and parent. Although the adults are in charge, and this is a directive therapy, the child is always shown kindness and respect. The child is never forced or coerced into participating, or into anything else. The child is never shamed or made to feel bad for their struggles, although these struggles are addressed. The main tools for engagement and buy-in for the child are playful engagement, fun, deep empathy, reflection, and truth.

11. M-MAT requires time, repetition and consistency to be effective. While M-MAT is an efficient therapy in addressing attachment injuries relative to other therapies, it is not a brief therapy. Therapists should ask caregivers to give them ten weeks to work with them and their child before judging if the therapy is working. By ten weeks, there should be evidence of change. There will likely, however, still be a lot of work to be done.

Additionally, consistency and repetition are crucial. The damage has been done, and at times self-perpetuated, over years. Repetition of the positive interactions, the structure, the re-storying, and the skill building is necessary to sustain change. New neural pathways are created through experience and strengthened through repetition. Just as repetition is important in building physical strength and skill, it is also important in building emotional strength.

The therapy structure in the parent/child session must be consistent. It will not work to use the M-MAT structure one session and not the next. When therapists have utilized the structure and the attachment narrative with attachment-injured children for one or two sessions, then returned to a less structured format, the report is usually some positive change at the end of, or immediately following, the M-MAT sessions, but then quick regression. Remember that the attachment-injured child's brain has been utilizing maladaptive patterns for a long time. The goal is to change those patterns. This requires repetition.

To sum up the key concepts:

1. The goal of M-MAT is to heal relational/attachment injuries to free the way for the child to develop to their full potential.
2. M-MAT is a two-pronged therapy, using both play and talk; healing through left and right brain functions.
3. M-MAT focuses on the parent/caregiver-child relationship and healing that relationship.
4. M-MAT is highly structured, allowing for safety, consistency and predictability.
5. M-MAT is a regressive therapy, going back to address early relational wounding.
6. M-MAT is a hierarchical approach, promoting safety and reducing anxiety through re-establishing appropriate adult/child hierarchy.
7. M-MAT is a directive therapy.
8. Attachment-based play provides the foundation for healing in M-MAT.
9. M-MAT creates a new story or narrative for the child that is adaptive and healing.
10. M-MAT is always respectful of the child and caregiver.
11. M-MAT requires time, repetition and consistency to be effective.

Therapeutic Stance

Throughout the therapy, the therapist wants to convey to the parent and child acceptance, curiosity and empathy. These are three of the four components described by Daniel Hughes, Ph.D., in his books on attachment therapy and Dyadic Developmental Psychotherapy as the central therapeutic stance in supporting healing for children and families. The fourth is playfulness, which is encompassed in the concepts of fun and play that are fully embraced in the attachment play portion of M-MAT and discussed in chapter 5: M-MAT Play.

Acceptance and empathy have long been recognized by most as fundamental to the therapeutic relationship. Humanist psychologist Carl Rogers identified unconditional positive regard and empathy as two of the three necessary elements of the therapeutic relationship to promote healing, the third being congruence or authenticity. With acceptance or unconditional positive regard, the child and parent are accepted for who they are and where they are in their growth and development. Voice tone is often as important, if not more important, than the words used in conveying a sense of acceptance. Acceptance or unconditional positive regard forms the basis for the therapeutic relationship in M-MAT with both parent and child.

Throughout M-MAT, the therapist uses empathy and deep empathy for the child and parent. The therapist wants to convey to parent and child an understanding of how they are feeling and where they are coming from. Empathy and deep empathy have been defined in many ways. For the purposes of M-MAT, empathy is defined as understanding how one would feel in someone else's situation. Deep empathy is defined as understanding how the other person feels in that situation. This definition of deep empathy is consistent with Carl Roger's definition of deep empathy as "...entering the private perceptual world of the other and becoming thoroughly at home in it."

For instance, if the therapist is a parent and can relate to some of the parent's struggles, the therapist can easily empathize with the parent. If the therapist has had experiences similar to the child's, they can empathize with the child in their struggles. Often, however, the therapist's perspective is quite different from the child or parent's.

As an example, a parent may say about their child, "He always tries to disrupt everything. He wants to make us miserable!" The therapist, however, may perceive that the child is largely having difficulty self-regulating in unstructured settings. It might be tempting for the therapist to immediately share their perception with the parent. It is more helpful, however, for the therapist to truly put themself in the parent's place. Whether true or not, the parent believes the child is trying to make them miserable. The therapist can consider how that must feel and explore what that means to the parent.

Of course, the therapist should also take care not to dismiss the parent's perceptions. In this example, a child may try to gain a sense of power and control by distressing their parent. Sometimes both may be occurring; the child has difficulty self-regulating in unstructured settings and also, at times, attempts to get a negative reaction from their parent. Regardless, parents need to be heard. If their child has very different behaviors inside the home than outside the home, parents may have struggled to get people outside the home to believe and hear them.

The therapist can use deep empathy to help parents be heard. The therapist can acknowledge the parent's view with a deep empathy statement such as, "It must be really hard to believe that your child is trying to make you miserable, trying to disrupt everything for you. I can imagine how hard that must be." The therapist can then give the parent a chance to respond and explore this. When the therapist makes a deep empathy statement, the therapist is not necessarily saying that they see the situation in the same way, but the therapist is acknowledging the parent's experience and saying that they understand it. The parent is then more likely to be open to the exploration of other perspectives or possibilities.

An example with the child might be when the child says of their parents, "They hate me!" The therapist may be aware that the parents care deeply for their child, but it is not useful to simply say, "No they don't. They love you very much!" Rather the therapist wants to view this as a distorted cognition that the child is carrying that is causing them a lot of distress. A deep empathy response would be, "Wow, that must be so hard to believe your parents, who should love and care for you, actually hate you. That would be very difficult to feel." Again, the therapist is not saying that it is true, simply that the therapist understands their perspective and how hard that must be. Deep empathy with the child not only allows the child to be heard, but also helps avoid power struggles and further entrenching the child in a negative viewpoint.

The talk portion of M-MAT can include a lot of questions by the therapist. An attitude of curiosity about the child and parent and their situation and responses demonstrates an interest in the child and parent and their experiences while minimizing defensiveness on the clients' part.

Curiosity is non-judgmental. Words like "I'm wondering about..." and "I'm curious about..." portray a sense of curiosity that minimizes defensiveness. Voice tone is very important and can convey a strong sense of curiosity. For instance, asking questions like, "So...are you saying that you have always loved Johnny?" with the right inflection of curiosity (higher pitch at the end of the question) can come across as a wondering on the therapist's part, rather than an inquisition or doubting the client.

So, with fun, acceptance, curiosity and empathy, the therapist joins with the family and child on a journey towards healing!

Structure

As noted previously, structure is an important, therapeutic part of M-MAT. This section provides an overview of the M-MAT session structure. Detailed interventions will be discussed in later chapters.

M-MAT consists of two types of sessions: Parent sessions and Parent/Child sessions. For the sake of consistency, it is important that the parent/child sessions occur at least weekly. Initially, it is helpful for the separate parent sessions to occur weekly as well. Later in the therapy, the parent sessions may be reduced in frequency, depending on parent need, as determined collaboratively with the parent. It may work well to have the parent session first, then, immediately following, have the child join the session for the parent/child component.

Parent Sessions

The parent sessions are an important part of the therapy. They provide an opportunity to address parenting concerns through the lens of attachment theory. Parents receive support, education and an opportunity to discuss challenges. Initially, parent sessions are weekly. It is a time when parents can review difficulties that have come up during the week, get the support they need and work on the parenting of their child.

Parents of attachment-injured children often feel like failures, so psychoeducation and support for the parents can be critical to the child's success. This component includes the therapist and at least one caregiver. It is even better to have both caregivers when there are two caregivers involved. If there are other individuals, such as other family members or childcare providers, who provide care for the child, it can be useful on occasion to include them in a session as well to provide psychoeducation and develop consistent strategies across settings for working with the child.

Parent/Child Sessions

Parent/Child sessions are the heart of attachment therapy. Through attachment-based play and therapy, the reparative, healing work for the child is begun. These sessions include the therapist, child and one or two caregivers.

The parent/child sessions are highly structured. There is a distinct beginning, middle and end to each session. The beginning and the end portions create the frame, which frames the middle talk section. Once the therapist has completed the assessment, if the therapist is not implementing the frame in every parent/child session, then they are not doing M-MAT. The parent/child session structure looks like this:

Beginning: Attachment-Based Play: The Frame Part 1
Middle: M-MAT Talk
End: Feeding and Attachment Questions: The Frame Part 2

Each of these parts has an entire chapter devoted to it, which describe the rationale, process and implementation in detail.

The following is an example of a typical parent/child therapy session:

Parent(s) and child come in and sit on the couch together. The therapist and family start with attachment-based play. These activities are designed to engage the child, provide nurturing and structure, encourage self-regulation, build trust and a sense of safety, and, most importantly, begin healing the attachment injury. These activities always include at least one of four attachment elements: touch, eye contact, mirroring and/or rhythm. They may include:

- Follow the leader games (the adults in the room always start as the leaders, but the child always gets a turn to lead as well). These games allow the child to learn to follow an adult's lead in an enjoyable and positive way, and gives the child the chance to be followed or mirrored by caring adults.
- Touch games or activities that are positive, non-intrusive and non-threatening such as clapping games, passing a 'touch' around the circle, thumb wrestling, or practicing a 'gentle touch' between parent and child. Positive touch is instrumental in healing attachment-injured children.
- Singing activities that are adaptations of familiar songs (e.g., "Row Row Row Your Boat," "Twinkle Twinkle Little Star" or "Rock a Bye Baby") that express caring and nurturing for the child.
- Eye contact games (e.g., peek-a-boo for young children, seeing how long parent and child can look at each other without breaking eye contact for older children).

Children are at times gently assisted in participating or encouraged to participate but are never forced to engage. Being playful often draws them in, and, on occasions when they choose not to engage, parent and therapist continue the play until the child is ready to re-engage. In some cases, the child will go through a phase of resistance to the therapy as they resist giving up control or feeling more vulnerable than they like, but this is usually short-lived. M-MAT attachment-based play is further defined and discussed in chapter 5: M-MAT Play. A list of attachment-based play activities can be found in Appendix A.

After the play, the therapist facilitates talk about whatever is appropriate. This may include addressing/ understanding past history (attachment narrative) and re-storying, skill building, psychoeducation, and/or addressing current behavior. Details on M-MAT talk can be found in chapter 7: M-MAT Talk.

The therapy session is concluded with the parent feeding their child a snack and parent and child answering positive, attachment-based questions. The therapist provides small crackers or some kind of treat (that the child likes and the parent agrees to), which the parent feeds to the child as child and parent answer questions such as "What is one time that you had fun with your child this week?" Questions are always positive and success oriented. Thus the session is ended on a positive note. If appropriate, the child also has the opportunity to feed the parent, thus supporting reciprocal interaction. This feeding activity is described in more detail in chapter 6: M-MAT Feeding and Questions.

These parent/child sessions can occur within the standard therapy hour: once a week for approximately 50 minutes. The length of parent/child sessions, however, should be guided by the child's tolerance for the therapeutic interaction and the material to be covered. Young children may do better with shorter, more frequent sessions.

Course of Therapy

Beginning Phase

The goals of the beginning phase of therapy are to assess, get the parents on board and have the child at least minimally cooperating.

The child usually comes to therapy due to the parents' concerns. It is often best to conduct the first assessment session with the parents alone, so they can speak freely in expressing their concerns, and the therapist can obtain a good history. It is also important to meet with the parents alone, without their child, to form a partnership with them in helping their child.

For continued assessment, the therapist can then see the child with the parents and possibly the child by themself. The therapist should conduct a thorough child and family assessment to fully understand the child and family needs. There are many good child assessments available, and it is beyond the scope of this book to go into detail regarding assessment. The therapist will want to make sure they observe parent/child interactions for attachment behaviors or lack thereof.

Once the therapist has completed a thorough assessment, if the therapist determines that M-MAT is appropriate, they then meet with the parents alone to discuss the assessment results, determine the level of parenting support needed, explain attachment and M-MAT and get buy-in from the parents. The therapist should also ask the parents to allow the therapist to handle behaviors in the parent/child sessions to avoid allowing children to power struggle with their parents or take control of the sessions. Let parents know that the initial work in therapy is on relationship building in session between them and their child. Parents are often relieved to be taken out of the disciplinarian role for this short period.

Additional parent-only sessions are designed around parent need. Therapist and parent can work on structure in the home, further psychoeducation, attachment-based parenting and parent support, as needed.

The beginning phase of the parent/child sessions should be very short, only one to three weeks. The initial Parent/Child sessions focus on engagement and activities oriented toward the child experiencing success and fun. Generally, sessions in the early phase of treatment involve more attachment-based play and less talk than in later treatment phases. The first session may be limited to attachment-based play and the feeding and questions portions. The initial goal may be simply to engage the child positively. The "Story of

Love" intervention, as described in the M-MAT talk chapter, is the first talk intervention and can be done in the initial phase of therapy. The therapist, in collaboration with the parent, is always in charge of the session, determining what activities to initiate.

Later in treatment, when the child demonstrates more integration of the self, the therapy will usually involve more cognitive work. Always, though, the structure of the therapy session is kept throughout, starting with M-MAT play and ending with M-MAT feeding and questions.

Sometimes therapists make the mistake of extending the beginning phase too long. When issues are not being actively addressed, the child and parent may get bored, the child will more likely act out in the session, and rapport can be lost. Parents have said that they addressed more substance in the first few weeks of M-MAT than they did in many months of other therapies. Once the child and parent are familiar with the structure, it is time to move on to the middle phase.

Middle Phase

The middle phase of the therapy is where the major work is done. Attachment play is continued throughout to address the non-verbal needs of the child. Additionally, issues are addressed directly through talk therapy. Historical issues are addressed first using the Story of Love followed by the Attachment Narrative as described in chapter 7: M-MAT Talk. Once the child's story has been told, with deep empathy and corrective cognitions, skill building and current behavior can be addressed more easily.

The therapist can expect some resistance from the child to surface in the middle phase of therapy. It is good to prepare parents ahead of time for this possibility. If the structure is consistent and maintained throughout, resistance tends to be brief.

In the parent only sessions, the therapist should be working with the parents to develop a support system, establish positive touch and one-on-one time with their child outside of the session, and strengthen parenting skills.

By week 10 of the parent/child therapy, parents should be reporting some positive changes in attachment and behavior for their child. This is not a brief therapy, yet there should be enough change or indicators at this point to give the parent enough hope and motivation to continue the therapy. If not, the situation needs to be reassessed. The middle phase of therapy can last anywhere from six months to several years, depending entirely on the progress and needs of the child and family.

Last Phase

The therapist will know that they are reaching the last phase of the therapy when the child is no longer trying to control the session, behaviors are under control, parents feel competent in parenting their child, and children and parents alike are demonstrating attachment behaviors with one another (spontaneous touch and eye contact, child seeking parent attention positively and looking to parent for safety and reassurance, parent providing positive attention, child demonstrating reciprocal behavior, etc.).

During this phase, the therapist wants to be sure that the parent and child are engaging in attachment activities outside of the therapy session. The therapy session should not be the only time that the parent and child engage in one-on-one focused time together. An adequate support system for the family should be well established. If the attachment between parent and child has been well restored/repaired, the therapist becomes superfluous.

Due to the nature of the therapy, however, parents and children can become attached to the therapist. The child, at times, can let go more easily than the parent because they are getting their attachment needs met through their parent. It is an important part of the parent work to help the parent develop an adequate support system. It may also be useful to taper the ending of therapy by meeting every other week for a period.

5

M-MAT Play: The Frame Part 1

Attachment-based play is the first part of the Multi-Modal Attachment Therapy (M-MAT) parent/child session and, along with M-MAT feeding and questions at the end, creates the frame for the session, framing the talk section in the middle. M-MAT play is implemented in every parent/child session.

What is Attachment-Based Play and Why?

Play has been described as the language of childhood and so is an ideal vehicle for communicating with children. There are varying definitions of attachment-based play. Attachment-based play is based on the earliest interactions between a parent and child. In M-MAT, attachment-based play is interactive and includes one or more of the following elements: touch, eye contact, mirroring and singing/rhythm.

Think about Peek-A-Boo, This Little Piggy, clapping games and rhymes and lullabies.

The most important purpose of attachment-based play is to heal attachment injuries by engaging and exercising attachment-related neural pathways, and through the child's experience of being cared for, loved and engaged. All the talk therapy in the world cannot take the place of the attachment-based play. How many clients, both child and adult, will say they know something in their head, but they don't feel it?

By using play, which includes touch, eye contact, mirroring and song and rhythm, with a primary caregiver, the child can have the physical experience of being loved and valued. This replicates the early experiences that support the development of those parts of a young child's brain that are related to attachment and relationship.

Attachment-based play engages the non-verbal parts of the child's brain. Using touch, eye contact, mirroring and song/rhythm would be considered a bottom-up therapeutic strategy in that it engages the body and senses in healing. Combined with M-MAT talk and M-MAT feeding and questions, M-MAT is a whole-brain approach to healing attachment injuries.

Attachment-based play serves several functions in the therapy: to facilitate appropriate attachment; to give the parents and child a break from the likely negativity in the relationship by disrupting negative cycles of interaction; and to set the child up to be more receptive to talk portions of therapy by reducing shame and defensiveness and increasing emotional regulation.

What attachment-based play is _not_ is board games, imaginative play, competitive games, or intellectual games. Other definitions of attachment-based play may differ from the one provided here. As defined in M-MAT, the play must include at least one of the four elements (touch, eye contact, mirroring and song/rhythm) and be interactive between caregiver and child. The four elements of M-MAT attachment-based play are further described below.

Appendix A contains a list of attachment-based play activities that meet M-MAT criteria. In addition to the activities listed in Appendix A, therapists can find attachment-based play activities online or in other resources. The therapist must always evaluate, however, if the activity described meets the criteria for M-MAT play before integrating it into the therapy.

Fun and Play in Attachment

When a child and parent are playing, laughing and having fun together, attachment healing is occurring. Neither child nor parent, at that moment, is in shame. It may take a few sessions for the child and parent to have those moments of fun, but they are priceless.

For the parent who has been struggling with their child every day and every moment, it offers some hope and some positive connection as well. For the child who sees life and relationship as a struggle, and adults, particularly parents, as people to be feared, it begins to create a different story. These moments are essential for healing and creating a new story. The new story is further extended and emphasized through M-MAT talk and the feeding and questions portions of the therapy.

Fun is a theme throughout M-MAT, not only in the play portion but in the talk portion as well. Moments of fun are emphasized and strung together to create a new narrative, and fun with family or caregiver is used as a motivator for the child when appropriate.

Elements of M-MAT Play

Touch

Touch is crucial not only to the development of attachment but also to overall child development and even survival. Failure to thrive has been linked in some cases to lack of touch, as have poor physical and mental development. One of the first ways an infant interacts with their caregiver is through touch. Parents use touch to soothe, comfort, cuddle and communicate with their babies. Touch is, by definition, connecting. The physical connection through touch is a good metaphor for the emotional connection children need. Attachment-injured children have not received adequate touch and/or have received hurtful touch. It is not unusual for them to avoid touch or to only use touch in aggressive ways.

Some people may question the use of touch in the therapy session with children who have experienced physical or sexual abuse. These children, more than any, need to know what good, positive, safe touch looks like. They may have no concept of positive touch. It is doing further injury to continue to deprive them of the positive touch they so desperately need.

It is important, however, to be sensitive to the child's response to touch, and it is important to create a high level of safety around touch in the session. It is helpful to state very directly to the child and parent that we only use safe, positive touch in session. It not only allows for safety for the child but also allows the therapist to redirect the child if they become physically aggressive.

Safety is further created by explaining and/or demonstrating with the parent first, asking permission when appropriate, and accepting a child's choice not to participate. It may mean working for a while with very non-threatening touch activities such as clapping games. For most attachment-based play, the therapist participates along with the parent and child. For more intimate activities, however, such as "Gentle touch" (see Appendix A), the therapist has the child and parent play while the therapist directs or stays out. This provides safety and models appropriate boundaries.

The importance of touch for attachment healing cannot be overemphasized. Every M-MAT session should have at least one activity that involves touch. Touch is preverbal, and since much of attachment injury is preverbal, it can touch and heal the most injured, vulnerable part of the child. Touch can also be encouraged throughout the session as appropriate. For example, a parent can be encouraged to hold or touch a distressed child or give a high five for a success during a therapeutic conversation.

Eye Contact

Another non-verbal conduit for connecting is eye contact. Think about the times in the supermarket when you have seen a young child with their parent, and the child makes eye contact with you...and just looks at you. They may look down and back up or look to their parent then back to you. Eye contact precedes verbalizations as a way of connecting. It is common for the attachment-injured child to avoid eye contact or use it only for expressing anger or control. The healthy young child uses eye contact with a parent for safety and reassurance. They will visually check back with a parent in an uncertain or strange situation.

Eye contact in session is again encouraged through games. Peek-a-boo, eye blink games, and staring contests are some examples (see Appendix A). Eye contact can also be encouraged in the talk portion of the therapy, when appropriate. It should, however, never be forced. Also, the therapist can coach parents to never insist on eye contact when they are angry. The, "YOU LOOK AT ME WHEN I TALK TO YOU!" statement is not useful. The child has to experience eye contact as positive in order to make connecting safe.

Mirroring

Mirroring activities help the attunement between parent and child. Parents and infants naturally mirror each other in their interactions and play. Imagine a parent and an infant interacting. Notice how they copy one another, smiling back and forth, making faces, and mimicking each other's vocalizations.

When a parent mirrors their child, it gives the child a felt sense of being seen, acknowledged, noticed, and creates attunement between parent and child. Children mirroring their parents is one of their primary ways of learning and growing.

In follow the leader/mirroring type activities, the parent leads first, then the child. It helps set the hierarchy and gives the child a chance to follow the parent in a non-oppositional way. The child gets an opportunity to lead as well and, thus, can have the positive experience of being mirrored by an adult.

Singing and Rhythm

Singing and rhythm are regulating, soothing and nurturing. It is one of the classic ways parents communicate comfort and love to their infant. Lullabies, for instance, are common throughout the world.

Rhythm and singing are regulating. They help the nervous system calm. By clapping in rhythm with their parent, the parent and child regulate and calm themselves together. This gives the child the opportunity to co-regulate with an adult, which creates safety and healing for the child.

Rhythm and singing are often integrated into play activities that also utilize touch, eye contact and/or mirroring. Examples include clapping games and Row Row Row Your Boat. Words to well-known children's songs can be changed to focus on positive messages to the child. See Appendix A for examples.

Some singing activities are designed specifically to meet the child's need for nurturing. Needless to say, the attachment-injured child has generally missed out on a lot of nurturing that occurs in healthier families. Singing, rocking and feeding are all nurturing activities that are included in M-MAT.

Guidelines for Implementing M-MAT Play

In M-MAT, attachment-based play is built into the structure of every parent/child session. It is part of the "Frame" of the session. Attachment-based play is engaged in at the beginning of each and every session, prior to any talk therapy. The second part of the frame, M-MAT feeding and questions, occurs at the end of the session, framing the session's middle, talk part.

The first thing to do to prepare for the attachment-based play is to get the parents on board. The therapist meets with the parents ahead of time and explains what they will be doing and why. Attachment-based play is generally regressive; that is, the child is allowed to be younger than their physiological age. The therapist explains this to the parents and makes sure they are OK with it. The therapist also tells the parents not to worry if their child does not go along at first. This is to be expected. They do not need to try to make their child participate. The parent and therapist engage in the activities with fun and enthusiasm, even if the child does not, periodically encouraging and inviting the child to participate. The therapist asks parents to allow the therapist to handle any behavior in the session while they work on developing and strengthening the child's attachment.

Sometimes parents are skeptical that their child will want to engage in the attachment-based play. They believe their child will feel it is too babyish. That is rarely, if ever, the case. The child is usually quite drawn to the play because it meets a deep inner need.

The therapy supports appropriate hierarchy through the play. The adults are in charge. In any activity, the therapist usually goes first, demonstrates, then the parent goes, then the child. The goal is that the child learn that the adults can be in charge, and it can be both safe and fun!

While the adults are in charge and the therapist should stay in control of the session, the therapist is not trying to control the child. Ultimately the child needs to be in control of themselves. This is important. The child choosing to join the play is psychologically very different from the child feeling coerced in some way to participate. Some parents may have difficulty with this, wanting to reward the child after the session if they participate or consequence them if they do not. This allows the child to manipulate in the session in order to gain the reward or avoid the consequence, then act out later. It does not allow the child to freely choose to participate, and may ultimately increase resistance and power struggles. This is contrary to the M-MAT model.

This response from parents may have to do with the feeling of being out of control. The therapist can emphasize with parents that they cannot control their child, only control their responses to their child in order to increase or decrease the likelihood of certain behaviors, and that the ultimate goal is for the child to gain self-control. Often, for the attachment-injured child, there is nothing the parent can or would want to do that is worse than what they have already experienced. By encouraging the child to participate, but allowing them to not participate, there is no power struggle. Then, once the child does choose to participate, it is a real choice to let go of a little bit of control and to trust the therapist and parent at least a little bit.

If the child chooses not to participate, the therapist engages in the activities with the parent, with enthusiasm, and periodically invites the child in, or, for the withdrawn child, can use the resistance to play peek-a-boo, etc. As long as the child is not doing anything destructive, the therapist stays focused on the activity with the parent, again inviting the child in periodically. The therapist needs to be sure the parent has been prepared ahead of time for this possibility. The child will not want to be left out of the fun for long! There are some activities, like singing to the child, that do not require the child's active participation at all. The therapist and parent can engage in these as a way to passively include the child.

Reasons the child may not participate could be that they are unsure of the safety of the situation, they do not want to give up control, or they are feeling uncomfortable because they are beginning to attach. These first two often happen in the first session. The latter is likely to occur several sessions in and is actually a sign that the therapy is working. Generally, the child will not hold out for long. Be sure to maintain the structure of the session through periods of avoidance. Do not make the mistake of discontinuing the play due to the child's reluctance.

The therapist uses tools of fun & enthusiasm to engage the child. The child can do no wrong. The therapist stays positive and provides encouraging, nurturing, positive responses even in the face of avoidance or resistance. The main tools of the therapist are enthusiasm and fun.

That being said, limits can and should be set around destructive or aggressive behavior. If a child becomes aggressive, e.g., hitting the parent or being overly rough in the play, it needs to be addressed immediately. The child will more likely be aggressive with the parent rather than the therapist. Using a positive but firm voice tone, the therapist can say something like, "Ah ah ah, gentle touch only! Let me show you!" The therapist can then demonstrate, and, if the child allows it, the therapist can gently take the child's hand and guide it to gently or appropriately touch the parent. As in general good parenting principles, the therapist wants to tell the child what they want, rather than focus on what they do not want.

As stated previously, the session should be structured, and the structure should be consistent throughout the weeks. This increases predictability and reduces stress and anxiety, making the child more able to participate in and process the therapy.

The therapist should always have the activities planned ahead of time. Indecision creates anxiety for the child and a need to control the situation. A leadership vacuum also creates anxiety for the child and a need to control. Have your activities written down prior to the session and reference this list during the session if needed. If a child asks for a particular activity in the session and it is not on the list, the therapist tells the child that they already have the activities planned for today, but maybe next week they can do it (if it is an appropriate activity). The therapist then puts it on the list for the following week.

This may seem controlling on the part of the therapist, but the therapist is working on letting the child know that the child does not have to be in control all the time (which is exhausting and anxiety producing for the child). The therapist is letting the child know that the adults are in charge and it is OK. The child can relax and be a child. Also, for some children, if they are given this control, they will try to take control of the whole session in a nonproductive way and derail the therapy altogether.

Be aware of what the child and parent may need in the moment. The therapist can alter plans if needed in session based on their own judgment. If the child seems to need a calming activity and the therapist does not have one planned, the therapist can still insert one. As another example, a parent may come into the session very frustrated with their child and feel unable to genuinely participate in a more intimate activity, like gentle touch. The therapist can then adjust plans accordingly.

For more complex activities, progress from simple to more complicated, stopping at the level appropriate to the child, thus encouraging success but adding a little challenge.

Repetition of activities within sessions and across sessions is not only OK, it is very good! For instance, the therapist may want to start sessions each time with the same clapping game to set the routine and provide a level of predictability. The activities are very short, and each can be done about three or four times in the session before moving on to the next activity. This allows the opportunity for mastery, comfort and familiarity with the activities.

Some activities can be increased in complexity either in the same session or in subsequent sessions. For instance, the therapist can use the same opening clapping game but, after running through it once or twice in session, if the child and parent have mastered it, the therapist can try it faster with the family, and even faster the time after that, all in a spirit of fun.

Children will benefit from being held and sung to multiple times throughout the course of the therapy. The therapist may only have a few different songs that they use, but they can mix them up and repeat them through the course of the therapy. It is useful to repeat singing a short song with the parent to the child three or four times before moving on to the next activity.

On the other hand, the therapist should be careful not to become too routine as they may lose engagement with the child. It usually works well to rotate through activities and introduce a new play activity, or a variation on a known play activity, every two or three weeks.

The therapist participates in most activities with the parent and child. This helps take the pressure off of the parent/child relationship, which is likely already strained, and helps the therapist build rapport with both parent and child. It also allows the parent to feel like they are not in this alone with their child. For children who are very reactive to their parents, the therapist engaging in the activities can help act as a buffer, increasing cooperation of the child. It further allows the therapist to demonstrate the activities, thus reducing the anxiety, for both parent and child, of not knowing what to do or doing it wrong. More intimate activities such as gentle touch or mirrors may be played by parent and child without the therapist, once the therapist has demonstrated, if needed.

Make sure each session has at least one activity involving touch. Touch is the cornerstone of attachment-based play. It is preferable to have at least one activity involving eye contact in each session as well.

In nurturing singing activities, such as "Rock A Bye Baby," it is not expected that the child will sing along, although it is fine if they do. This is an opportunity for the adults to provide unconditional nurturing to the child.

Have fun! Stay positive and out of power struggles, utilize resistance, and have fun! Fun increases bonding and reduces shame. When a child is having fun, the child is not in shame, which allows them to be better able to connect with their caregiver and also allows them to better participate later in the talk portion of the session.

Keep a positive tone of voice. This is very important. Children will respond to tone of voice before they respond to words. The therapist's voice tone should convey enthusiasm and fun! To see what this looks like, observe or imagine a well trained, experienced preschool teacher. Note the positive tone of voice the teacher uses to corral the children into circle time: "OK, It's circle time! Come sit on your mats!" Enthusiasm is conveyed, and the children are more likely to pay attention and comply.

Direct, do not ask the child. Asking the child if they want to participate sets the therapist up for a "no" answer, which will ultimately make it harder for the child to participate. The skilled preschool teacher imagined above does not ask the children to come sit on their mats. She does not plead. She directs them, but with such a positive voice tone that resistance is reduced.

Similarly, in session, the therapist directs with positivity. The therapist does not make the mistake of asking the child if they want, for instance, to play a clapping game. Instead, the therapist says with enthusiasm something like, "We're going start today with a clapping game! It goes like this..."

Do not try to verbally process the attachment-based play. The play is experiential and designed to address preverbal injuries. Trying to process the play verbally may move the child into an older state and out of the experience, and it may also increase resistance.

Be patient and expect resistance. The more disturbed the attachment, the longer it may take for the child to relinquish control. It is not unusual for a child to go along at first but then go through a period of avoidance. This is a signal that the child is getting too close for comfort and is a last-ditch effort to maintain distance and/or control. This is a sign of progress. Stay consistent and positive. This phase does not usually last long.

Reflect after each session on what worked and what didn't. What type of activities does the child most need at this time in the therapy? Does the child need to start the session with a more regulating activity? Does the child need more focus on nurture? Consider each session as feedback for planning the next session.

To summarize the guidelines for implementing attachment-based play in M-MAT:

1. Attachment-based play is a part of every session.
2. Get the parents on board.
3. Establish hierarchy.
4. There is no attempt to control the child.
5. The child can choose not to participate - Parent and therapist continue with the play inviting the child in regularly.
6. The therapist uses tools of fun & enthusiasm to engage the child.
7. The child can do no wrong.
8. Set limits around aggression.
9. The session should be structured and the structure consistent across sessions.
10. Always have activities planned ahead of time.
11. Be sensitive to parent and child needs in the moment, adjusting activities if needed.
12. For more complex activities, progress from simple to more complicated, stopping at the level appropriate to the child.
13. Repetition of activities within sessions and across sessions is not only OK, it can be very good!
14. The therapist participates in most activities.
15. Parent and child may play more intimate activities, such as gentle touch, without the therapist (once the therapist has demonstrated if needed).

16. Each session should have at least one activity involving touch and one with eye contact.
17. Nurturing activities such as singing do not have any expectation of the child's active participation.
18. Have Fun!
19. Keep a positive tone of voice.
20. Direct, don't ask.
21. Do not try to verbally process attachment-based play.
22. Be patient and expect resistance.
23. Reflect after each session on what worked and what didn't, and plan the next session accordingly.

What To Do When...

- Child refuses to play - That is OK. Play with the parent in a spirit of fun and with enthusiasm. Prepare the parent well in advance of the parent/child sessions that this may happen, and that it is OK, and that the therapist and parent will continue to engage in attachment-based play with one another while periodically inviting the child in. Ignore any distracting behavior by the child, but continue to invite them to play. Usually, children will not sit out for too long because they do not want to be left out. Remember, fun and enthusiasm are the M-MAT therapist's tools for engagement!

- Child becomes overly agitated/excited in the play - Integrate more regulating/self-calming activities such as rhythm games and breathing activities. Also, stop/go games (like Fast/Slow clapping in Appendix A) can help children learn to regulate after excitement. Do some quiet singing activities with the parent holding and rocking the child at the end of the play portion to help them regulate. The therapist may find the child gets overactive standing up, so the therapist may choose only sitting activities for a while until the child has learned to regulate their energy level better. Use each session to plan the next session in determining what works best for the child. If an activity seems too activating for the child, move on to the next activity.

- Child becomes aggressive in the play - Remind the child, "Gentle touch! We only use gentle touch in here." Physically and gently redirect the child to gentle touch if needed, and as the child will allow. Usually, if the child becomes aggressive, it will be with the parent. Often the child will allow the therapist to take their hand and physically demonstrate gentle touch with the parent using the child's hand, saying something like, "We touch gentle, like this." Early on in the therapy, the therapist should talk about using only gentle and safe touch in the session.

- Child becomes inappropriately physically affectionate with the therapist - This is a good opportunity to teach boundaries around touch. For example, if a child jumps into the therapist's lap, the therapist can gently remove them and say something like, "Oh, you know, we don't know each other very well. When you don't know someone very well, you can give them a handshake, like this..." (demonstrate). The therapist might ask the parent, "Whose lap is it OK for (child) to sit on?" Parents, maybe grandparents or other close family members, might be identified. The therapist can then engage the child and parent in a short conversation around this.

- Child uses touch inappropriately with caregiver - For instance, a child starts kissing a caregiver's neck in a way that feels inappropriate. This can happen particularly with sexually abused children. Again with a positive voice tone, limits are set, parents are asked to tell the child what would be an appropriate way to touch them (e.g., a hug or a high five). Some children hug in a way that does not feel appropriate, holding on too long or too tightly. Sometimes the hug can feel controlling. In this case, it is good to teach an appropriate hug, i.e., ask for the hug, then hug for a count of 4 or 5, then release. This can be done briefly in the moment. If there is a persistent problem, it can be further addressed in the talk/skills building section of the therapy.

- Child is highly reactive to touch - Slow down. Ask permission to touch. Give the child the option to opt out of touch. Again, continue with the parent, modeling and demonstrating the safety of the activity. Start with less intense types of touch activities like clapping games and high fives. See if the child prefers firm or light touch. Consider the possibility of sensory integration issues and refer to an occupational therapist specializing in sensory integration if appropriate. Also, be sure that autism spectrum disorders have been ruled out.

6

M-MAT Feeding and Questions: The Frame Part 2

M-MAT Feeding and Questions is the third and last part of the Multi-Modal Attachment Therapy (M-MAT) session. It is the second part of the frame and, along with attachment-based play at the beginning, frames the talk section in the middle. M-MAT Feeding and Questions is implemented in every parent/child therapy session.

What are Feeding and Attachment Questions and Why?

Feeding is a fundamental part of caring for young children. In M-MAT, it represents nurturing and the parent's ability to take care of the child's needs. It also engages more of the child's senses in the therapeutic process. Taste and smell are inextricably linked to early memories. By using feeding, we can engage yet another part of the child's brain in the therapy. Feeding is also soothing and grounding, supporting the child in leaving the session in a well-regulated state.

In M-MAT, the feeding ritual is tied to attachment questions. These attachment questions are based on the idea of "stringing pearls" from Narrative Therapy. The idea is to identify discreet moments (pearls) and to string them together to support an alternative narrative to the dominant, oppressive narrative. Attachment questions are designed to support the attachment between child and caregiver.

Each week, at the end of the session, the therapist asks about positive experiences and appreciations between parent and child, past, present and future, creating a new story or narrative. The narrative that the therapist is working to develop and support is that the parent enjoys and values their child, and the parent/child relationship can be fun and positive. These questions are asked at the end of the session as part of a feeding ritual, and, thus, the session always ends on a positive note.

Attachment Questions

Sample attachment questions include:

> What is a time that you remember having fun with Suzie when she was just a little girl?
> Suzie, can you remember a time when you had fun with your (mother, father, family)?
> What is a time recently that you and Suzie had fun?
> Can you think of a time this week that you two had fun together?
> What is something you look forward to doing with Suzie?
> Suzie, what is something you look forward to doing with your mom?
> What is something you appreciate about Suzie?

Suzie, what is something you appreciate about your mom?

What is one thing Suzie did for you this week?

What is one thing your mom did for you this week?

Mom, how about when Suzie is a bit older, maybe a teenager or even an adult, what is something you look forward to doing with her?

Suzie, what is something you look forward to doing with your mom when you are a lot older?

The therapist is also trying to re-story the idea that the parent does not care about the child. Children often have no idea or awareness of all that their parents do for them as a matter of course, and attachment-injured children may be particularly blind to this. The following questions are useful in addressing this:

Mom, what is something that you do to show Johnny that you care about him?

Johnny, what is something you think your mom does that shows she cares about you?

Moms do a lot of things for their kids, and most of the time we don't even notice! Mom, what is one thing you do for Johnny?

Johnny, what is one thing your mom does for you regularly?

It is also good to define coming to therapy as something the parent does for the child:

And I know something else she does for you! She brings you here every week and works together with us!

Process

In M-MAT feeding and questions, questions are asked alternating between parent and child. The parent answers the question first, then the child. This allows the parent to model for the child and to verbally give to the child first. Each time a question is answered by either parent or child, the parent feeds the child a small snack. The snack is agreed to ahead of time by the parent, making sure that it is something the child likes. Small tasty crackers tend to work quite well. Parents sometimes playfully fly or swim the little crackers or snacks into their child's mouth. The child's boundaries are always respected, however, and some children may not be comfortable with this. They may, for instance, prefer to have their parent put the snack in their hand, and that is fine.

At some point in the therapy, the child will often want to feed the parent as well. This may be due to the child wanting to reciprocate, which is a positive sign of progress, or because the child wants more control. Either way, if this works for the parent, then the feeding alternates between parent and child, with the parent always feeding the child first (maintaining an appropriate hierarchy).

Repetition. Repetition. Repetition. Repetition of questions week to week is OK and desirable. For instance, most weeks, if not every week, the therapist should ask about a time the parent and child had fun together. Sometimes they may have a hard time remembering a time that week. If the therapist noticed them having fun in the session, perhaps during the attachment-based play, the therapist can suggest that as a possibility. The therapist can also extend the timeline to, "How about any time in the past?" It is only necessary to do three or four questions per session. The repetition over the weeks is enough to make an impression, and the snack/feeding is symbolic.

Sometimes the child has a hard time coming up with answers. It is OK, then, to focus on asking questions only of the parent while they feed the child. As with infants, the focus is on the parent nurturing and feeding the child, both literally and figuratively. As the therapy progresses, it is likely that the child will be better able to participate in answering questions.

Every parent/child session ends with this ritual. It usually only takes a few minutes, and the session always ends on a positive note. Thus, each parent/child session is framed by the attachment-based play at the beginning and the feeding and attachment questions at the end. This frame creates a therapeutic container for the talk section in the middle.

7

M-MAT Talk

Multi-Modal Attachment Therapy (M-MAT) Talk occurs in the middle of the therapy session, framed by the attachment-based play at the beginning and the feeding and attachment questions at the end.

What is M-MAT Talk and Why?

While attachment-based play is largely non-verbal and experiential, M-MAT talk engages the thinking, verbal part of the brain. Thus, by integrating both attachment-based play and talk, M-MAT attempts to treat the whole child, endeavoring to engage as much of the brain as possible in healing.

For M-MAT, the term "talk" is used broadly to include not only talk but therapeutic games and activities commonly used with children. For instance, a therapeutic board game or drawing activity would be appropriate in M-MAT talk.

M-MAT talk can be divided into four different categories: Re-Storying, Skill Building, Psychoeducation and Addressing Behavior. Throughout the talk therapy, the therapist is always trying to speak in a way that supports a new, healthier narrative for the child: that the child is valuable and loved and cared for.

Much attachment injury occurs pre-verbally for the child, but the child has grown and with that growth is the incredible cognitive growth that occurs during early childhood. Unfortunately for the attachment-injured child, much of that growth has occurred around a faulty template of how the world works, based on the child's early experiences. Maladaptive beliefs become the filters through which the child views the world and around which cognitive development is organized. These beliefs are tied to the child's survival, so they are held tightly, though often not consciously. The Re-Storying part of M-MAT talk addresses these faulty beliefs head on.

Research is also clear that early neglect and abuse cause deficits in the child's functioning and cognition, including difficulty self-soothing, identifying and expressing emotion, deficits in cause and effect reasoning, and social difficulties. Skill deficits are addressed through skill building talk, games and exercises.

Psychoeducation is used throughout the talk portion of M-MAT, but there are a few areas the therapist will want to address specifically: shame vs. healthy guilt, parent/child roles and clarifying responsibility. Opportunities to address these issues may come up naturally in session, or the therapist may plan to address them specifically.

Also, due to the maladaptive beliefs and skill deficits, the child is likely exhibiting behavior problems. It is often these behavioral difficulties that have brought the child in to therapy in the first place. The child's maladaptive beliefs and skill deficits can both generate a lot of behavior problems and interfere with the parents's effectiveness in addressing those behaviors. A negative spiral can occur in the interactions between parent and child as the parent tries to address the child's behavior. The Addressing Behavior portion of M-MAT talk is geared at disrupting that negative cycle, helping the child to understand discipline differently, and providing the parent with additional parenting tools.

Specific interventions in each of the four categories (re-storying, skill building, psychoeducation and addressing behaviors) are described below. How to integrate these into the therapy over time is further clarified in chapter 9: Putting It All Together, including a sample therapy timeline.

Therapists with training in other specific therapeutic tools or modalities, such as EMDR (Eye Movement Desensitization and Reprocessing) or EFT (Tapping/ Emotional Freedom Technique), may want to integrate these into the talk portion of M-MAT. This will be discussed further at the end of this chapter.

Re-Storying

Many of the ideas for re-storying derive from Narrative Therapy concepts. The idea is that the child has created a storyline for their life based on their interpretation of events. This storyline then invests new events with the same meanings and themes of the maladaptive or dominant storyline. Any events that do not fit into the original or dominant storyline are often simply not seen or noticed. For instance, a child who was abused or neglected when young may have created a storyline that goes something like: I was a bad kid, so people hurt me, and no one loved me; I am still bad, so no one will ever love me, they will only hurt me. These themes or story lines are often not conscious for the child, yet they drive the child's behavior. One can see how this storyline or theme would create difficulties for the child attaching to a caregiver.

It is also easy to see how this child might become easily dysregulated because they see themselves as bad, which creates intolerable feelings of shame and anxiety. It does not take much to trigger these difficult feelings (shame, hurt, anger) and push the child beyond their ability to cope. Contributing to this is the fact that the child's coping/self-soothing skills are often minimal due to their early history.

Furthermore, if a child feels they are bad, they will do bad things, even when not dysregulated, creating a lot of discipline challenges. Then, if a caregiver tries to discipline the child, the child will interpret it as, "I'm bad" and, "They are trying to hurt me (with the discipline)." It will be very difficult for the child to see that the caregiver is trying to help them through discipline or consequences, and so a vicious cycle develops.

The underlying dominant, maladaptive story must be addressed early in the therapy in order to be effective in the rest of the work.

The goal then of the Re-Storying talk portion is to help the child re-write their story. In the talk portion of M-MAT, this is done primarily through the Story of Love, the Attachment Narrative, What Do Babies Need, Storytime, and the Heart of Hearts interventions as described below.

It should be noted that the stringing pearls concept discussed in chapter 6: Feeding and Questions, and the weekly experiences in the attachment-based play are also part of the re-storying for the child.

Story of Love

The Story of Love is the first talk portion of M-MAT in which the therapist engages the child and parent. Remember, the talk portion is sandwiched between the attachment-based play and the feeding and questions. The story of love should be the only topic of the talk portion in this session. This first talk session will start with attachment-based play, move on to the story of love, and end with feeding and attachment questions. This may be a short session, under the standard 50 minutes, which is fine.

There is a great deal of power in speaking about love, yet, as therapists, we do not often do it. In telling the story of love, the therapist, with the parent, is defining the love of parent to child as unconditional and ever present, everlasting. The story of love is told from the past, to the present, to the future.

This story is told as a conversation between parent and therapist with the child in the room. Nothing is expected of the child. It is good to encourage the child to sit with the parent, but if they don't, it is OK as this hypervigilant child will be listening to every word. The child can sit with the parent, wander around the room or fidget with a toy. The fact that nothing is expected or demanded of the child during this intervention is important because it reduces the child's anxiety, which will allow them to absorb the information better.

It is also good to brief the parent ahead of time, but this intervention can usually be accomplished successfully without the parent having prior knowledge. A reasonably healthy parent will be able to answer these questions appropriately. If the parent is unable to answer these questions appropriately, then that is a sign that the parent is not ready to participate in M-MAT.

The therapist both prompts the discussion with questions and highlights the desired answer by repeating/reflecting what the parent says. The repeating/reflecting is important because it allows the child to hear the information not only from a parent, against whom the child may have a lot of defenses, but from the therapist as well. Repetition is also important as one tool in getting the new story and new information through to the child. The following is an example. Of course, the timeline will vary depending on whether the therapist is speaking to biological parents or adoptive parents or relative caregivers, and parent answers will vary, but the idea is the same. The therapist should use a leisurely pace in their speech and not run through the questions too quickly:

Therapist: (to parent) So I'm just wondering how much you love Jaylen? Do you love them this much (hands close together), this much (hands further apart), or this much (hands and arms spread far apart)?

Parent: Parent will often say something like "I love them to the moon and back!" or "More than my arms can stretch" or "This far" (stretching their arms as far as they can).

Therapist: Oh, you love them...(repeating what the parent said).

Parent: Yes!

Therapist: Well, I'm curious, when did you start loving Jaylen? When is the first time you felt that love for Jaylen?

Parent: When I first saw their face, I just fell in love with them. I knew they were my baby!

Therapist: Ah, so when you first saw Jaylen's face, you just fell in love with them. You knew that they were your baby!

Parent: (confirms)

Therapist: OK, so you first loved Jaylen when you first saw their beautiful face...But, I'm wondering, you know, when children are toddlers, 2 or 3 years old, they can be so active, running around, getting into everything! Did you still love Jaylen then?

Parent: (affirms)

Therapist: OK, you loved Jaylen when you first saw their face, and when they were a toddler, running around getting into everything, you still loved them. Toddlers can certainly be really cute. How about when they were a little older? Say six. No longer a little toddler. Did you still love them then?

Parent: affirms

Therapist: OK, so you loved Jaylen when they were little little, and also when they were 6 years old. But I'm curious about now. Now that Jaylen is 10 years old, do you still love them?

Parent: Of Course! I'll always love Jaylen!

Therapist: Of Course! You'll always love Jaylen! OK, OK, I hear you...But, you know, teenagers can be a little difficult. When they are a teenager, maybe wearing funny clothes or getting their hair cut funny, do you think you will still love Jaylen then?

Parent: (affirms)

Therapist: Are you sure?

Parent: (confirms)

Therapist: OK, so you loved Jaylen when you first saw their face, you loved them when they were little, you love them now, and you'll even love them when they're a teenager. But what about when Jaylen is a grown-up? When Jaylen grows up, maybe is as tall or taller than you, and maybe moves out of the house and is an adult, say, 22 years old, will you still love them then?

Parent: (affirms)

Therapist: OK, so you're saying, even when Jaylen is all grown up, even when they are as tall, or maybe even taller than you, even when they are no longer a child or baby, you will still love them?

Parent: Oh, Jaylen will always be my baby! I'll always, always love them!

Therapist: OK, Got it!...Hmmm...if Jaylen grows up and should decide to have children, and they may or may not, but if they do, that means their children would be...?

Parent: my grandchildren...

Therapist Ohhh... so that means you...would be... Jaylen's children's grandma? (this seems particularly helpful for children who are adopted as it fully confirms them as part of the family).
Parent: (confirms)
Therapist: When do you think you will stop loving Jaylen?
Parent: Never!
Therapist: Are you sure?
Parent: (confirms)
Therapist: Does that mean that you will always love Jaylen?
Parent: (affirms)
Therapist: Forever and ever?
Parent: (affirms)
Therapist: No matter what?
Parent: I will always love Jaylen no matter what!
Therapist: Wow, you'll always love Jaylen no matter what. I am hearing that you will always, always love them.
Parent: (affirms)
Therapist: OK, well that is good to know. Thanks for letting me know that. Let's move on to the last part of our time together today...

All the while, the child is listening. This is followed by the M-MAT feeding and questions part of the session.

This one session is not likely enough to convince the child that they are loved or change their narrative, but the Story of Love, combined with attachment-based play and feeding and questions, is a good beginning!

Attachment Narrative - The Child's Story

The attachment narrative is perhaps the single most important intervention in the talk portion of M-MAT. It forms the core upon which the child's new story develops.

The attachment narrative is a re-telling of the child's story from birth to the present. During the attachment narrative, the therapist, parent, and child revisit all the child's important life events. The therapist and parent help the child make sense of their story and correct cognitive distortions or misunderstandings of the meanings of the events. Along the way, new meanings are created.

The child may actively participate in the telling or not, depending on age and the child's readiness and ability to participate. Most children will participate at least a little in the telling of their story, but there is no pressure to do so. They can be invited, but not required.

Be clear that the Attachment Narrative is not the same as the trauma narrative in TF-CBT (Trauma-Focused Cognitive Behavioral Therapy). The trauma narrative in TF-CBT focuses on processing trauma, going into a lot of specific detail regarding a traumatic event. The attachment narrative takes a much wider view, reviewing the whole life of the child from birth. The attachment narrative recounts both difficult and positive events in the child's life. Any trauma the child has experienced is discussed in the attachment narrative in the context of the child's life but in a much more general way. The details are not explored, but the meaning of any such event is.

Going into the details of trauma is not necessary in M-MAT and can trigger PTSD symptoms or re-traumatize the child. It is the meaning the child has made of the trauma that is causing the child the most difficulty in their life. This is what is focused on and addressed in the attachment narrative.

The attachment narrative is done before skill building interventions because the child is not likely to be cooperative with skill building early in the therapy. The issues discussed in the attachment narrative are already present for the child, and the attachment narrative often provides the child with some relief. As stated, details of trauma are not explored, as it is not necessary, and this helps avoid re-traumatizing the child. How events are addressed will become more evident in the example below.

The attachment narrative, or child's story, is told during the talk portion of the therapy session, after the attachment-based play and before the feeding and attachment questions. The attachment-based play, along with the feeding and questions, constitute the frame of the therapy session, which provides a therapeutic container for the talk portion. This promotes soothing and emotional regulation for the child and ensures that the session ends on a positive note.

The child needs to make sense of their experiences. It is OK to use leading questions to direct the conversation. The therapist uses questions, comments and reflection to highlight and enhance particular aspects of the story in order to create a healthier storyline or theme.

The therapist works with the parent and child to tell the child's story from birth on, including both positive events and stories about the child, and traumas and other events (e.g., separations) that could disrupt attachment. The therapist leads the discussion of feelings associated with the event for both parent and child. The therapist and parent correct errors in thinking and clarify responsibility and fault throughout. The therapist elicits an apology from parent to child for not protecting the child as each trauma is discussed, or for other attachment disrupting behavior, such as parental substance abuse. The therapist facilitates the conversation about how things are different (safer, better) now.

The therapist should cover:

• Child is not at fault - Children carry a lot of shame and responsibility for their parent's poor behavior. They feel that they are bad, otherwise these things would not have happened to them. This is a core belief that needs to be addressed both directly and indirectly.

- Empathy and normalization for child's feelings - The child may not be able to express their feelings. It is OK to say things like: "That could be so hard for a little kid" or, "Gosh, that must have been so confusing."

- Apology parent to child - Even if the parent is not the one responsible for the neglect or abuse (such as an adoptive parent), this is important. This removes the shame from the child and reinforces the idea that the child is not at fault. All children deserve to be well loved and cared for and protected. The apology acknowledges this and holds the adults accountable. This supports healing for the child. An example of how to do this with an adoptive parent is given below.

- How the parent has tried or is trying to help and support the child - The child is often quite oblivious to the ways in which the parent has been there for them or has tried to support them. It does not fit with their dominant maladaptive story, so parents' protective or supportive behavior is misinterpreted or not seen at all.

- Why things are different now/why child is safe now; includes parent, child, and situational changes - This helps reduce anxiety and changes the present story from "I am not safe" to "I am safe."

- What the child can do if the child ever feels unsafe - Included in this should be going to the parent and/or other supportive adults. The child may not know how to do this as it may not have been an option in their early experience. This changes the story from "I'm on my own, no one can help me" to "I can get help, I have grown-ups in my life who will help and protect me." It is also empowering for the child to have some concrete strategies that move them from the powerless infant place to a place of power.

The adults are responsible for clarifying the story. The child participates as able. The therapist can support the parent in providing nurturing during the narrative (e.g., encourage the parent to hold or hug their child, rub their child's back, etc.) as needed and appropriate, and as the child will allow.

Some of the tools used during the narrative are:

* Repetition and reflection to highlight desired points (corrected cognitions).
* Psychoeducation.
* Having parent verbally reinforce corrected cognitions.
* Bringing in child's experience of babies/young children to explore ideas around responsibility.

The therapist should talk to the parent ahead of time about the attachment narrative. It is important that parents know that both difficult and positive things will be discussed, so they are psychologically prepared. Explain the rationale for the attachment narrative. Explain the process. Let them know that the therapist will ask questions and highlight events and answers, but they should feel free to add anything they feel is important.

Introduce the attachment narrative in the session with parent and child as the child's story. For a child who is able and willing to participate, the conversation moves between parent and child, as each is able to fill in relevant parts of the child's story. Start with where the child was born. The therapist can ask the child this question first, then default to the parent if the child cannot answer or does not know. This gives an easily defined, objective starting point to the child's story. While the child's story starts well before they were born with the family history and pregnancy, it is sufficient for the purpose of the attachment narrative to start with the birth of the child. The story then moves through the child's life, year by year.

The following example gives some of the therapist's questions and cues for an adopted child with her adoptive mother:

- Introduce the topic:

  Today we are going to tell the story of Sarah!
  Sarah, do you know where you were born?...Oh, you were born in San Antonio!
  Now you would have been too young to remember anything about your birth, but have you ever heard any stories about the day you were born?...
  No?...
  Mom, do you know anything about Sarah's birth?...
  Was she born in a hospital?...
  Do you know, after she was born, where she went home to?...Who was in the home that she went home to?...
  OK, so after she was born, she went home with her mother to her grandmother's house.

- Include positives such as:

  I bet you were a cute baby! Mom, do you have any pictures of Sarah when she was a baby?...Sarah and Mom, do you know any stories from when Sarah was just little?

- Introduce difficult subjects:

  I know some hard things happened when you were still
  very little. Mom, what were some of the hard things that
  happened when Sarah was little...Sarah, what do you
  remember about what happened?

- Give the opportunity for sharing of information (may be
  documented in court or child welfare documents):

  ...Oh, so Sarah's biological mom and grandma both
  struggled with addiction... (discuss difficulties the
  biological parent may have had that affected the child,
  but never put down biological parents. To attack the
  biological parent is to attack the child).

- Provide psychoeducation:

  ...Gosh, when parents are struggling with addiction, they
  usually have a really hard time providing their babies
  with what they need...That can be so hard for the babies
  (empathy)...
  When babies or little kids don't get what they need, they
  can be so sad and angry and confused. Sometimes they
  even think that it's their fault!

- Provide more psychoeducation and correct the presumed
  cognitive distortions:

  ...It is a funny thing, the way little kids' brains work, they
  think whenever something hard or bad happens it is
  their fault, but you know, it is never the baby's or kid's
  fault. Never, ever! Babies are just babies that need and
  deserve to be taken care of and loved and protected.

- Have the parent reinforce the correction:

    Sometimes kids think if they were just better kids or better babies, their biological mom might have been able to care for them better or not done drugs in the first place.
    Mom, do you think it is in any way Sarah's fault that her biological mom wasn't able to take good care of her?...Or did drugs?...
    That's right. It is never the child's fault!

- Bring in the child's experience of younger children/babies.

    Sarah, do you know any one-year-olds?...Do they cry sometimes?...Is it OK if they cry or fuss or get into things?...
    That is right, that is just what little kids do!
    Would it ever be OK to hurt (name of child Sarah knows)?
    Of course not! She is just a baby!
    What if the grown-ups around her were having problems and didn't take care of her right? Would it ever be her fault?
    Of course not! Grown-ups are responsible for their own behavior! Babies and little kids are just babies and little kids! They are never responsible for a grown-up's behavior!

- Move towards an apology parent to child, even with an adoptive parent who was not there at the time:

    Mom, I know how much you love Sarah. You must feel so bad that she was not cared for right when she was little... (give a chance for parent's response).

You know, even when it is not our fault, when we weren't there, as parents, we feel so bad when our children get hurt. I bet you wish you could have been there, that you could have made sure Sarah was cared for like she deserved to be! (space for parent response).
Can you look at Sarah and tell her how sorry you are that she was not well cared for when she was just little...that you weren't able to be there for her?
Parent: Sarah, I am so sorry you weren't cared for right when you were little. I wish I had known you then. I wish I could have been there for you and kept you safe.

- The therapist might prompt the parent to give Sarah a hug at this point, if the parent isn't already doing so, and it feels appropriate:

  Mom, do you want to give Sarah a hug?

- Focus on how things are different/better now. Talking about difficult things has likely raised the child's anxiety. This not only continues to create a new story but also reduces the child's anxiety:

  How are things different now than they were when you were a baby?

- Repeat, reflect and highlight the answers that are part of the new story:

  That's right; you are older and bigger now! You can get help if you need to!
  Mom, how are things different/safer now than when Sarah was a baby?

- Again, repeat, reflect and highlight the answers that are part of the new story:

> That's right; you are able to take care of Sarah. You don't do drugs, and you always make sure Sarah has food to eat and a safe place to sleep. You are able to take care of Sarah!

After some further elaboration on how things are different now, this may be a good stopping point for the talk part of this session. The attachment narrative can be told in pieces over multiple sessions. The therapist wants to be sure to end each talk portion on a positive note. The therapist can now move the session to the feeding and questions:

> Well, I think we have talked enough for today! We'll keep telling Sarah's story next time we meet. Let's move on to our snack.

The feeding and questions portion is positive, grounding and soothing, preparing the child to re-enter the world. In the next session, the attachment narrative will pick up where it left off in the timeline of the child's life.

Throughout the attachment narrative, the therapist also focuses on, highlights and expands the elements that support a new and positive understanding of the role of the parent in the child's life. For instance, when working with a mother and child, if part of a story is that the mother called the police when she found out that abuse was occurring, the therapist would highlight this protective act on the mother's part by asking questions and inquiring further about the meaning of this. For instance, the therapist might say:

> So you mean that as soon as you found out, you called the police?

How come you called the police when you found out?
That's right; it is illegal for an adult to hurt a child!...
People understand that it is the grown-ups who are responsible when something like this happens. The grown-ups know better, and children are just children and should not be hurt. That's why it is illegal for grown-ups to hurt children (psychoeducation).
So, Mom, you must have known that it was not Sam's fault...
And why else did you call the police?
Oh, so you did not want Sam to be hurt any more...
You wanted to keep him safe...
That's right; you wanted to protect him...
And why did you want to protect him?...Of course, because you love him and never want to see him hurt. Sam deserves to be safe and protected...

This, then, is a good opportunity to explore the mother's feelings and move towards an apology:

You know, when something like this happens, moms usually feel pretty bad that they had not been able to keep it from happening. I bet you feel pretty bad that this happened to your little one...
That's right...so even though you did not mean for this to happen, and it wasn't your fault, can you let Sam know how sorry you are that (name of perpetrator) hurt him; that you couldn't protect him? Can you look at Sam and tell him how sorry you are?
Parent: I am so sorry that you were hurt. I'm so sorry that I wasn't able to keep him from hurting you.

Highlight again the protective act:

You are so sorry he was hurt and you couldn't protect him. But, when you did find out, you were able to protect Sam. When you called the police, you were protecting him.

The therapist now moves on to "how things are different now," asking questions about why the child is safer now and elaborating. These should include:

- How circumstances have changed.
- How the parent is keeping the child safe.
- How the child can help keep themselves safe.
- What the child can do if they ever feel unsafe.

The attachment narrative is continued every week in a linear timeline until the child's story is told up to the child's current age. The child is encouraged to ask questions of the parent as the story is told. It can be very useful to go through the child's life year by year, and, for each year, ask the parent and child what they know or remember about that year in regards to the child and family. For instance:

Kayla, what do you remember about being 5 years old?
Mom, can you remember anything that happened the year Kayla was 5 for Kayla or the family?

After exploring the year's event and before moving on to the next year, ask the parent and child if there is anything else:

Mom and Kayla, before we move on to the next year, is there anything else important about Kayla's 5th year? Anything we forgot?

When I have worked with teens and parents, it has been fairly common for previously undisclosed abuse or trauma to surface in the attachment narrative. Checking in with parent and child before moving on allows a second chance for clients to share something that they may have held back to this point.

The Attachment Narrative should include the following life events:

- Child's birth
- Who the child lived with
- Positives about the child
- Changes in living situation
- Birth of sibling(s)
- Trauma and neglect

In regards to siblings, there is sometimes a theme or distorted cognition that there is not enough love in the family to go around, or a sibling is more loved than the child. This can be addressed during the narrative with questions such as these:

> You know, sometimes kids think that their parents don't have enough love for all of their children. Mom, do you have enough love in your heart for both of your children? Are you sure?
> If you love Mikaela, are you able to love Sam as well?

Sometimes, particularly with older children, there will be a need to revisit events later in the therapy that were not fully explored in the attachment narrative or about which the child has further questions.

It is not unusual for parents or caregivers to become emotional or tearful during the attachment narrative, particularly when discussing emotional issues such as their child's early abuse or neglect. This is an excellent opportunity for the parents to model appropriate emotional expression and reassure their child of their emotional strength. It is also a good opportunity to reinforce the parent's caring for their child. Through their parent's modeling, children can learn that it is OK to be sad and OK to express emotion.

Children may feel overwhelmed in the face of their parents' emotions and may feel they need to take care of their parents. The therapist lets the child know that it is OK to feel, and that their parent is strong and can handle their feelings. The therapist:

- Acknowledges the emotion.
- Acknowledges how the child may be feeling in the face of that emotion.
- Expresses why, as a therapist, they are not worried about the parent.
- Has the parent express to the child that they are OK.
- Explores the meaning of the emotion, tying it into the parent's caring for the child and other M-MAT talk themes.

This would look something like this:

Therapist: I see, Mom, that you are getting emotional. You know, sometimes when kids see their parents get emotional, they are worried that their parents are not OK. I know, though, that you are OK. I know that you can feel strong emotions and still be OK.
Therapist: (To child) I'm not worried about your mom because I know how strong she is, and I know it is OK to have feelings and that your mom is OK.
Therapist: (to Mom) Mom, what are you feeling?
Mom: I'm feeling sad.

Therapist: Oh, you are feeling sad. Can you let Rico know that even though you feel sad, you are OK?

Mom: Rico, I feel sad, but I'm OK.

Therapist: Can you tell Rico why you are feeling sad? What is sad for you?

Mom: I'm sad that things were so hard for you when you were little. I wish no one had ever hurt you. I wish I could have been there for you then.

Therapist: (reflecting) You wish no one had ever hurt Rico. You wish you could have been there for him.

From here, the therapist can explore with parent and child the M-MAT themes of fault and guilt (not the child's fault), parent's caring for the child, apology parent to child, and/or how things are different now.

If the child tends to do a lot of self-blaming, it may be important to also have the parent reassure the child that it is not the child's fault that the parent is sad. The child is not responsible for the parent's emotions.

If the parent has some responsibility for what occurred to the child, then this is a good time to move to an apology from parent to child. This is therapeutic for both the parent and child.

Storytime

Throughout history, stories have been used to gently teach and instruct. The human mind seems to use stories to organize and make sense of the world. So why not use stories in the therapy that speak to connection and positive parent/ child interaction?

I have used a number of picture books with parents and children. Parents or therapists may feel that picture books are too young for their child, but that is OK. As noted previously, attachment-injured children are generally at a younger emotional age than chronological age, and many of the interventions in M-MAT are regressive. Additionally, picture books have the advantage of being engaging, short, and to the point.

What I have found most useful has been to have the parent and child snuggle together while I read them a story. The therapist could also have the parent read the child the story. This may be particularly useful for parents who are not in the habit of reading to their child if that is something the therapist would like them to do at home. The therapist could read the first time or two to model, then allow the parent to read to their child.

I have some favorite picture books that explore the enduring bond between parent and child. You can find them in appendix B. The therapist can periodically slip in a book during the therapy, rotating through them. Or if the child seems particularly enamored of one of them, it can become a staple in the therapy. Reading picture books can be a really nice activity to transition the child and parent to the feeding and questions portion of the therapy, or to fill in when there is extra time.

Like many M-MAT interventions, the therapist doesn't need to process the story with the child and parent. They can just allow the story to do its part. Of course, if the child spontaneously talks about the story, that is fine and provides an opportunity to reinforce the themes of the story.

Heart of Hearts

Heart of Hearts is a strategy that can be used as needed throughout the therapy. In helping the child re-write their story, the therapist and parent are trying to communicate that there is a valuable, amazing child underneath the lies of the dominant or dysfunctional story. We can speak directly to that inner healthy child. If used sparingly and appropriately, children generally do not balk at this because it does resonate with their inner needs.

The therapist wants to be careful not to use this in a way that negates the child's experience. The therapist can do this in part by being tentative and owning the idea through "I think..." statements, and not directly contradicting something the child just said.

For instance, the therapist and parent, in the presence of the child, may be discussing how the parent would love to have the child fully engaged with the family and be able to have good relationships with everyone in the family. The therapist might say, "You know, I think, in her heart of hearts, Jenna wants that too. I believe, in her heart of hearts, Jenna wants to be part of the family, wants to have a good relationship with everyone."

It is important that the therapist does not require the child to state this or confirm this because that sets the child up for a "no" response and an argument or power struggle over the issue, further entrenching the child in an opposite view. The therapist just makes the statement and moves on.

What Do Babies Need?

This intervention is helpful when the child is in a new home setting, such as an adoptive home. It helps both child and parent understand why the child is having such a hard time trusting and accepting love and support from their new parents or caregivers. It also explores the idea that the new situation is different from the old situation, supporting a new story for the child.

The therapist pulls out a baby doll to illustrate. The following are some of the questions and psychoeducation that the therapist provides. The questions are asked of the child with the parent providing support:

Here is a baby; what do you think babies need?

That's right; they need food, and they need a home.

What else do they need?

Do you think babies need love?

How do you think people show their babies they love them?

That's right; they take care of them. They change their diapers and hold them when they cry, they make sure they are fed, and they play with them.

Did you know that babies, to be healthy and happy, need to be held and touched?

That is one of the ways parents let their babies know that they love them. Even before the baby can understand their words, the parents hold and hug their babies in good gentle ways.

Babies don't have words yet, so how do babies let their parents know that they need something?

Is it OK for a baby to cry?

Yes, of course it is OK – that is the way they let their parents know they don't feel good.

When a baby cries and their parent picks them up and takes care of them, the baby learns that they can trust their parent. The baby learns that their parent is there for them.

For inhibited attachment: When that doesn't happen, the baby is not sure if they can trust grown-ups and sometimes doesn't think that any grown-ups can really help them.

For disinhibited attachment: When that doesn't happen, the baby might start to look to any and everyone, even strangers, to get what they need. They don't know what it is like to have a special person, a parent, really take care of them.

So how are things different now? Do you think (your adoptive parents) can take care of you?

How do they take care of you?...

(To parent) What are some of the ways that you take care of Michael?

What are some of the other things you do for him?

That's right, you...

And, another thing I know you do for him is to bring him here and meet with Michael and me.

So your mom is different than your biological mom was. What other ways is she different?

Does she do drugs (if the biological parents did drugs)?... (Sometimes the child will express a concern here that, for instance, their adoptive mom has a glass of wine at night. It is important to explore these concerns with child and parent and how it is different to allay fears. Of course, make sure there isn't an actual substance abuse problem.)

This intervention is ended with how things are different now.

Skill Building

The skill building portion of M-MAT is largely the same as in other child therapies involving skill building activities. Skill building activities may include games, role-play and discussion. Do not confuse skill building games with attachment-based play, however. The parameters, focus, and methods are different. Skill building falls into the talk portion of M-MAT, occurring in the middle of the therapy session, framed by the attachment-based play and the feeding and questions sections.

In the course of the therapy, skill building should occur after the story of love and attachment narrative, and once the child is somewhat cooperative in the session. If the therapist tries working on skill building too early, there is a good chance that the child will not cooperate, or will be too anxious to absorb the information or participate fully.

Five skill building areas that should always be included with attachment-injured children are self-regulation/self-soothing skills, feelings identification and expression, communication skills, problem solving and boundaries. Social skills can also be useful for many attachment-injured children.

There is a lot of information and many exciting resources available to therapists for teaching these skills. Many child therapists will have their own favorites. I, therefore, will only briefly describe below some of the strategies I use regularly in these areas. Therapists are encouraged to find their own go-to strategies.

Self-Regulation/Self-Soothing

Self-Regulation/Self-Soothing skills are taught and practiced throughout the course of therapy. Here are a few:

• Breathing - It is important to teach breathing skills as breathing is critical to self-regulation. Some possible ways of teaching these skills are:
  - Teaching through psychoeducation, demonstration and instruction of belly breathing or diaphragmatic breathing.
  - Breathing together: practice breathing with therapist, parent and child holding hands. The parent and child follow the therapist as the therapist raises their arms up and breathes in, then lowers their arms down and breathes out. The raising and lowering of the arms helps encourage diaphragmatic breathing. This exercise also allows the therapist to easily pace the breathing, while

the hand holding and synchronizing of the breath with parent and child are nice attachment pieces.

- Flower and candle: Have the child and parent practice breathing in through their noses, as if they are smelling a flower, and breathe out through their mouths, as if they are blowing out candles.
- Breath counting: Count child and parent through breathing, "In two three four, hold two three four, out two three four."

• Progressive Relaxation - Attachment-injured children are often too anxious to participate well in guided imagery relaxation, but progressive relaxation, with the focus on tightening and relaxing various muscles moving up and down the body, can be effective.

• Five Things - This is a mindfulness exercise that uses the senses to help a person get grounded and focused in the here and now. It can help reduce anxiety and help a child move away from being triggered. Have the child say five things they see, without thinking about it, just what they see at the moment. It is OK to repeat. Then five things they hear. Then five things they feel. The child then says four things they see, hear and feel. Then three things, then two, then one. If five things seem like too many for the child, you can start with three things. The therapist and parent can model for the child.

• Physical Exercise - Physical exercise can help the child regulate in the moment and over the long term. Work with parent and child to identify physical activity that the child can engage in regularly and specific things they can do when the child finds themself getting frustrated or tense, such as jumping jacks or running around the yard. Practice in session when appropriate.

• Sensory Activities - Some children may find running their hands through sand or dry beans or another medium soothing. Rubbing a soft piece of velvet or a smooth stone might bring comfort to other children. Some children may calm with a weighted blanket. Work with the parent and child to identify soothing sensory activities.

Therapists should identify with clients several strategies they are comfortable with and then practice them regularly in session. Repetition is important in teaching the skills and increases the chance the child will recall and implement the skills when stressed. The therapist may help the parent and child create a list or poster with their chosen strategies that can be easily accessible in the home. If the child is able to be cooperative with the parent, have them practice together at home. The more the child can practice, the better.

Feeling Identification and Expression

Once again, there are many resources available for teaching these skills. Some useful interventions include:

• Feelings Charades - Have a list of eight to ten feelings for all to see, for reference, and cards with those same feelings on them. Have each person, in turn, pick a feeling card, and act out that feeling while the others try to guess the feeling.

• Feelings Matching Game - Have pairs of feeling cards. Mix them up and place them face down. Like any memory game, take turns picking pairs and trying to find a match. If someone gets a match, they share a time when they felt that way, and they keep those cards. They can choose not to share a time they felt that way, but then they have to put the cards they picked back where they got them. Contrary to other memory games, if the person gets a match, they do not go again. The play passes on to the next person so that more people get turns. Sometimes a child may purposely not pick matches to avoid sharing feelings. In this case, use the Feeling Cards game, described below, the next time.

• Feeling Cards - Have a set of feeling cards. Spread the cards with just the backs showing and have the parent pick a card. The parent then tells the child a time they felt that way, starting with, "I felt happy when..." Then the child tells the parent a time they felt that way. Next turn, the child picks the card, but, again, both parent and child tell about a time they felt that way. The play goes back and forth until all the cards are gone. The therapist can also participate if it would help to model for the child and/or parent. This activity can be extended to include reflective listening skills described further in communication skills.

• Feeling Cards In-the-Moment - Use the feeling cards during the session. Once the child is familiar with the cards, they can be used in the moment to help the child express themselves. For instance, if the child experienced a difficult event during the week, the therapist can pull out the feeling cards and go through them one by one, asking, "Did you feel (emotion) when that happened?" and separating out the cards that they acknowledge. At the end, the therapist can reflect back the feelings, "Oh, so you felt sad and mad and scared when..." The therapist can further help the child explore their feelings by asking further questions like, "What was scary about that for you?" or "What was the saddest part for you?" It can also be a good opportunity to talk about mixed feelings and how one often has several different, and possibly conflicting, feelings at the same time.

Once the therapist has modeled this for the parent, they can encourage the parent to do this with their child, both in the session and at home.

Communication Skills

The therapist can keep this very simple with the below exercise and in-the-moment coaching.

- Reflective Listening Skills - Have the child tell the parent a time they had fun, starting with, "I had fun when..." Have the parent reflect back what they heard, starting with "I heard you say that you had fun when..." Let the child confirm or clarify. Then have a parent say a time they had fun and coach the child to reflect back in the same way. Early in the therapy, start with easy/comfortable feelings like fun, happy, excited. When the child and parent seem ready, the therapist can include more challenging feelings like sad, mad and disappointed. The therapist can have the parent and child pick from feeling cards to determine which feeling to use. Always be sure the child and parent reflect the feeling they heard when reflecting back to the other.

- In-the-Moment Coaching - The reflective listening skills exercise gets the child and parent ready for in-the-moment coaching during other discussions to use these skills. For instance, a child might express anger about something that happened in the home. The therapist can then coach the parent to reflect back what they heard the child say before responding themselves, and vice versa. This can help facilitate understanding between parent and child and can sometimes slow down an otherwise volatile conversation.

Boundaries

Attachment-injured children often have unclear boundaries with peers and/or adults. There are many activities and guidelines for teaching boundaries to children. Some useful ones are listed below.

• Boundaries Circles Psychoeducation - Explain circles of familiarity wherein a diagram with concentric circles is labeled from most intimate (family) in the center to least intimate (strangers) on the outside. Facilitate discussion regarding appropriate behavior with those in each of the circles, including appropriate touch.

• Boundary Walk - In this exercise, explain how different people have different comfort levels with physical closeness, and that their comfort level is also determined by where people fall in the boundary circles (see above). In this exercise, have two people face each other about 5 feet apart. One of the people is the controller and instructs the other person to take a small step forward, then evaluates their comfort level. If comfortable, they then direct the other person to take another step forward. This continues until the controller has decided that they have reached the limit of their comfort level. The two people then repeat the exercise with the other person as the controller. They can then see how their comfort levels are the same or different.

   In a session with the therapist, parent and child, start with the parent and therapist in order to demonstrate and role model for the child, then the parent and child, and finally the therapist and child.

   This can also be done with the individuals side to side rather than facing each other, and it can be noted how the comfort level can be different side to side rather than face to face. Discussion can then ensue regarding the differences in comfort level and how to respect other people's boundaries and have other people respect our boundaries.

• Touch Psychoeducation and Role-Play - Include discussion of good touch/bad touch and role-play of how to stay safe, set boundaries with others, and get help if needed.

Problem Solving

Practicing problem solving skills helps children to slow down and think through situations. It also reinforces cause and effect thinking as possible solutions are evaluated for possible outcomes. Problem solving techniques are the same in M-MAT as in any other therapy. The therapist helps the child and family generate possible solutions, evaluate the options and role-play solutions. In role-playing, it is usually helpful to the child for the therapist or parent to role-play and model the solution before asking the child to do so.

One format I use for problem solving is POP CAR:

1) **P**roblem - Identify the Problem
2) **O**ptions - Brainstorm Options
3) **P**ossible Outcomes - Consider Possible Outcomes of Ideas
4) **C**hoose
5) **A**ct
6) **R**eward - Reward Yourself

As an example, suppose a child is being excluded by a couple of their peers:

Problem:
Being excluded

Options:
- approaching and talking it out with peers
- yelling at peers (during brainstorming, write down all ideas without judgment)
- playing with someone else
- getting help from an adult
- not going to school
- helping the teacher during break time

Consequences:

Go through the above ideas and discuss what might happen in each situation.

Choose:

Will play with someone else.

Act:

Act on the decision. Role-play ahead of time if helpful.

Reward:

Child pats themselves on the back, maybe saying something like, "Good for me!" Parent gives a high five, or other congratulatory response, for making the attempt.

Problem solving can be practiced in session with made-up scenarios as well as real-life scenarios. Parent and child can also practice problem solving skills at home. Repetition, as always, is important. Over time, not only can the child gain proficiency in problem solving, but they can further learn that they can be effective in the world and understand that their actions have consequences.

Social Skills

Depending on the child's functioning and needs, social skills can be useful. The therapist may choose to focus on peer social skills if social stressors are causing distress or concerns in the child's life. As the child becomes more securely attached to their primary caregiver, the child will likely become more competent in peer relations and more resilient in the face of peer challenges. Like other areas of skill building, there are many resources for therapists to draw on. Some useful interventions are as follows:

• Role-Play - For social skills, role-play real-life situations that the child is experiencing. Allow the child to play a peer, and the parent or therapist can play the child, modeling different types of behavior and responses, depending on the concern. The parent may need modeling and coaching to be effective here. The child then plays themself, practicing the different responses.

• CBT Role-Play - For children who are highly reactive to their peers, implement CBT (Cognitive Behavioral Therapy) role-play. First, the therapist provides psychoeducation on the CBT triangle and how thoughts, feelings and actions are connected. Then, the therapist acts as the child in the role-play, stating out loud different ways of thinking, leading to different behavior. For instance, if it is a peer teasing situation, the therapist might say aloud, "Oh, they hate me! Something is wrong with me! Everyone hates me!" and acts out resulting behavior. The therapist then acts out a more adaptive response in the face of teasing, saying something like, "Oh, wow, they seem to be having a bad day! I wonder what their problem is?!" The therapist, parent and child then discuss how the two responses feel different and lead to different behavior. The child then will have the chance to demonstrate and verbalize in role-play more adaptive thoughts and responses.

Psychoeducation

While psychoeducation is embedded throughout the talk portion of the therapy, there are a few specific topics that are useful to discuss when appropriate in the therapy as follows.

Shame vs. Healthy Guilt

Attachment-injured children are often acting from a place of shame. It is important to distinguish between healthy guilt and shame. Healthy guilt is the idea that I have done something wrong, and I feel bad about it. Shame is the idea that I did something wrong, and, therefore, I am bad.

Healthy guilt allows a person to evaluate the situation, make amends if needed, and do something different the next time. Shame gives the person no place to go. If the child did something bad because they are bad, then there is nothing further for them to do. Being bad gives the child no options other than to continue to be bad. As discussed previously, often one of the core beliefs of attachment-injured children is that they are bad. If they do something wrong, this just confirms their "badness," and children who feel they are bad, act badly.

In session, when discussing behavior, it is important to make the distinction between shame and guilt. This can be plainly and simply explained to both parent and child, as the therapist continues to separate the child from their behavior.

Parent/Child Roles

The other area that is ripe for discussion is parent versus child roles. For severely neglected children, there was no distinction in roles. They often had to fend for themselves, and sometimes siblings. They may have had to take care of getting food, finding a place to sleep and getting their basic needs met. This, as one might imagine, produces a lot of anxiety in a child.

The situation now may be very different. The child may be in a different home, or their parents may have been able to step up into the parenting role. The child, however, is still acting from survival instincts, trying to take care of everything and make sure that everything is OK. They may have no idea of appropriate child/parent roles.

This can be addressed throughout the therapy by exploring what is different now. That is, exploring how the parenting situation is different and how the parent is capable of taking charge and taking care of things. The parent can be encouraged to reassure the child that they are capable of handling whatever needs arise.

It also can be addressed through direct psychoeducation on the role of parent and child. Clarify through discussion with parent and child the parent's roles and responsibilities and the child's roles and responsibilities. The therapist might briefly discuss what roles are, and ask parent and child what they feel their own roles and responsibilities are as parent and child. The therapist can ask questions to the parent and child such as:

> Is it Mom's job or Jeri's job to make sure there is food in the house?
> That's right! And Mom, is that something you can do?
> And as a kid, what is Jeri's job?" (answers may be to go to school, grow, learn, play, do chores...)

Brainstorming and making lists of the roles of family members may be useful. The child can be reassured that they no longer need to worry about a lot of things and that the parent(s) will make sure these things are taken care of.

It can also be useful to use the metaphor of a sports team wherein everyone works together, but the parents are the coaches; the parents are ultimately in charge and always have the final say.

Opportunities to explore parent/child roles and the question of who is in charge in the family may come up repeatedly in the therapy. Remember that repetition is good, and it will take time for the child to understand and adjust to their role and fully trust that their parents will really take care of things.

Clarifying Responsibility

The question of responsibility is addressed throughout the discussions of the child's history. It is always emphasized that children are never responsible for the behavior of adults. Responsibility, however, may be a difficult concept for the child to fully grasp. They may take responsibility for things that they are not responsible for, such as a peer calling them a name, while, at the same time, not take responsibility for their own behavior. Therefore, it can be useful to address the concept of responsibility independent of the child's history through the Who's Responsible intervention.

- Who's Responsible - In this psychoeducation exercise, the therapist has a list of situations prepared. The situations should not use the names of people actually in the child's life. The therapist may write these out on cards and have the parent and child choose cards to discuss, or the therapist may simply present the situations to the parent and child for discussion. Discussion then ensues on who is responsible for what. For example, one situation may be as follows:

Jessie called Hannah stupid, and Hannah hit Jessie. Who is responsible for what?

This may seem like an easy question to answer, but the child may feel that Jessie is responsible for Hannah hitting him, or that Hannah may have done something that made her responsible for Jessie calling her stupid. In the discussion, it can be clarified that Jessie is responsible for calling Hannah stupid, while Hannah is responsible for hitting Jessie. It can be pointed out that only Hannah can be responsible for hitting Jessie because only Hannah is inside of Hannah's body. Only Hannah can control what her hands do. Only Jessie can be responsible for calling Hannah stupid because only Jessie is responsible for what comes out of his mouth.

The therapist can then move on to the next situation, or can allow the discussion to expand into discussions about feelings vs. actions (e.g., Hannah may have felt like hitting Jessie, but that is not the same as hitting Jessie); impulse control; and problem solving. What could Hannah have done instead? What could Jessie have done instead?

The types and complexity of the situations presented can be tailored to the needs of the particular child.

Addressing Behavior

Much of the child's behavior (home, school, community) is addressed through separate work with the parents when possible (Please see chapter 8: Working with Parents and Other Caregivers). While it can be important to address behavior in the child/parent session as well, it is important that the child/parent sessions NOT become about the child's misbehavior. Too much focus on behavioral problems with the child can actually increase the behavior. With very young children, perhaps 4- and 5-year-olds, it may not be necessary to discuss the child's behavior in the parent/child session at all. In this case, the parent/child session is focused on attachment and skill building, while support around behavior is provided in the parent only sessions.

For most children, however, it is important at times to discuss their behavior in session; otherwise, it can become the elephant in the room, particularly if more extreme behaviors are occurring. It can also be useful for setting goals in the therapy and monitoring progress as well as providing opportunities for problem solving.

It is important that there be an expectation set in the therapy of no secrets. Part of the goal in discussing behavior is to help the child be able to tolerate those discussions. Thus, it is particularly important for the therapist to take a stance of acceptance and curiosity. Shaming and blaming are avoided, and understanding the behavior, what drives the behavior, and how to address the underlying issues or emotions, become the goals.

The therapist wants to unravel the behavior sequence to its source and the likely maladaptive thoughts or beliefs that support it. It is important to hold off addressing outside (home, community, school) behavior in the session until after the story of love and attachment narrative have been explored, and the child is reasonably cooperative with the attachment-based play and feeding and attachment questions (the frame) and skill building activities.

During the initial period of therapy, the parent sessions can be very important in supporting the parent regarding the child's behavior, particularly if the child is displaying extreme behaviors. In the parent/child sessions, behavior can be addressed through discussion, problem solving, externalizing anger, success focused questions and 'no set to yes set' interventions.

Discussing Behavior in the Parent/Child Session

Whenever discussing behavior in an M-MAT parent/child session, the therapist wants to achieve the following:

- Clarify causality through questions - Attachment-injured children often have difficulty connecting their behavior to the consequences of their behavior, thus impairing their ability to learn from their experience.

- Explore how behavior causes problems for the child - Often, parents and others try to tell the child how their behavior has caused problems for others (parents, family, peers), but early in the therapy the child may not care, and may even be pleased to be causing others distress due to their anger and defense against their own pain, and/or a sense of power from their effect upon others. So, initially, focus on how the behavior is causing problems for the child, and try to move the child to a place of enlightened self-interest.

- Explore what need(s) the child is trying to meet.

- Clarify and explore how parent and child want the same thing - In reality, any reasonably healthy parent wants their child to be happy and well and able to participate and be a part of the family. They want them to have good relationships and good experiences. Children, ultimately, want the same thing.

- Clarify parental intention (i.e., that the parents are trying to help the child) - The child's perception is often that the parent wants them to be miserable, particularly when imposing any kind of consequence. The parent's intention in imposing consequences, however, is ultimately to help the child learn and to be healthier and happier.

It is important to acknowledge the child's attempts and improvement in engaging in the discussion. The therapist shapes the child's behavior towards constructive conversation using verbal praise or acknowledgment. The therapist also uses curiosity and questions to help the child make the cause and effect connection between the child's behavior and consequences, natural or otherwise. This is to help the child move from a victim position to an empowered position where they actually do have some control in their lives. Empathy and deep empathy are used as needed to build connection and validate the child's experience. Finally, the therapist externalizes the behavior, emphasizing that the behavior is the problem, not the child.

As an example, a child may come in upset that they were unable to participate in a family outing. Underlying this upset is the idea that the parent does not like them and wants to exclude them. Now, before addressing this, the therapist, parent and child engage in the attachment-based play. If far enough along in the therapy, the child will be used to this and will likely engage. As always, though, they can choose not to, and the therapist and parent still engage in the play.

The talk part of the session then may go something like this:

Mom: Brian is mad because he didn't get to go to ice cream with us last night.
Therapist: Oh, Brian is mad about missing ice cream. How come Brian missed ice cream last night?
Mom: Well, we were all getting ready to go, then Brian decided he didn't want to put his shoes on and threw a fit!

Brian: NOT AH! YOU WOULDN'T LET ME PUT MY SHOES ON!

Mom: Brian, that is not true. I even brought them down for you!

Brian: You hate me! You're the meanest Mom! You don't let me do anything!

Therapist: Oh, that is so hard Brian! To think that your mom hates you and doesn't let you do anything! It must hurt to think that! (deep empathy)

Brian: (silence)

Therapist: Mom, it sounds like Brian has some ideas that don't feel good. Can you imagine how hard it must be to think your parent doesn't love you?

Mom: That must be really hard Brian. I can understand how hard that must be.

The therapist uses deep empathy with the child, and encourages the parent to do the same. This parent has already learned about deep empathy and goes right along. The deep empathy allows the child to be heard and avoids an argument about whether or not the parent loves the child, which could cause the child to become more entrenched in the idea that they are unloved.

Therapist: It sounds like it is difficult for Brian to feel your love for him. Mom, I'm curious, you said you even brought him his shoes. Why did you bring him his shoes?

Mom: Because I wanted him to get ready to go with us.

Therapist: So you wanted him to go with you?

Mom: Yes, of course.

Therapist: OK, so Mom, you wanted Brian to go and even brought him his shoes?!

Mom: Yes.

Brian: (brooding silence)

Attachment-injured children often have a deficit in cause and effect reasoning. With any maladaptive behavior, the therapist clarifies in the session, through questions, the cause and effect of consequences related to the behavior. The therapist initially emphasizes how the behavior is causing problems for the child as opposed to how it is causing problems for the family and/or parent. If the child is angry or needing a sense of power and control, the child may be pleased on some level that the behavior is disruptive to the family or parent. Therefore, the therapist moves the conversation to how it is causing the child a problem as so:

Mom: But Brian threw a fit, wouldn't put on his shoes, and made us all have to wait for him! (Parent describes how a behavior was disruptive to the family.)
Therapist: OK, so I understand how that fit caused some problem for the family, but how did it cause a problem for Brian?

Then continue the conversation elaborating and clarifying the consequences of the behavior for the child, being careful to separate the child from the behavior and externalize the behavior:

Mom: Well, Brian had to stay home with Nana and couldn't come to ice cream with us.
Therapist: So Mom, are you telling me that if Brian had put his shoes on, not thrown a fit, he could have gone to ice cream with you?
Mom: Of Course!
Therapist: And Brian, are you saying you wanted to go to ice cream?
Brian: (silence)
Therapist: So what I am hearing, Brian, is that you could have gone to ice cream if you had put your shoes on. I

wonder why you chose to not put them on? (Emphasizing the child's choice here, and thus his power.)

Brian: (silence)

Therapist: So, Mom, would you have liked Brian to be able to go with you?

Mom: Well yes, but not if he is going to throw a fit!

Therapist: OK, but in the best possible world, you would really like it if you could take your little boy to ice cream?

Mom: Yes, I would love to be able to have Brian join us!

Therapist: Why would you want Brian to join you?

Mom: Because I love him. He's part of the family.

Therapist: You love Brian and would love to have Brian join you! And if he hadn't thrown a fit about his shoes, he could have gone?

Mom: Yes, of course!

Therapist: Then you could have had fun together! (emphasize fun)

Mom: Yes.

Therapist: OK, so what I am hearing is that you would love to have Brian go to ice cream with you, and Brian would like to go to ice cream too, so you both want the same thing! Isn't that great that you both want the same thing! Now we just need to figure out what is getting in the way...Hmmm...It seems like that fit got in the way! That fit sure kept you from getting what you both wanted!

So here the therapist has clarified the cause and effect (fit resulted in child not going to ice cream), emphasized that the parent and child want the same thing, and also externalized the behavior (it was the fit that was the problem, not Brian). The therapist can then explore what needs the child was trying to meet through the fit.

Therapist: Hmmm, I'm really curious why Brian didn't want to put his shoes on...Brian, how come you didn't want to put your shoes on?

The therapist gives the child a chance to respond. If the child does not respond, or if the response seems ingenuine:

Therapist: Mom, do you have an idea as to why Brian didn't want to put his shoes on? (Parents often have good insight into their child's behavior.)

Mom: I think he was mad at me because he didn't want to stop playing and put away his toys.

Therapist: Oh, so maybe anger got in the way (externalizing anger). It can be hard to have to stop playing and put away toys when you're in the middle of something (empathy). That can be really frustrating.

Brian: I was making a star station!

Mom: Brian was building with his blocks and there were pieces everywhere. I asked him to pick them up before we left.

Therapist: Ah, so you wanted Brian to pick up his blocks, and Brian wanted to save his star station. I wonder if we could come up with a solution...Let's think about how we could have solved the problem of Mom wanting Brian to clean up and Brian wanting to save his star station...

We are now ready to begin problem solving. It could be done informally, or with more structure. Here is an example using POP CAR.

1) **P**roblem - Identify the Problem
2) **O**ptions - Brainstorm Options
3) **P**ossible Outcomes - Consider Possible Outcomes of Ideas
4) **C**hoose

5) **A**ct

6) **R**eward - Reward Yourself

Problem:

Brian wanted to save his project and mom asked him to pick it up.

Options:

- ask mom if he could save it
- scream and yell (during brainstorming, write down all ideas without judgment)
- offer to tidy up the blocks not being used

Possible Outcomes:

Go through the above ideas and discuss what might happen in each situation.

Choose:

Ask mom if he could save it and offer to tidy up.

Act:

Act on the decision.

Reward:

Yay for me! High five from mom.

You could role-play in session the child enacting the chosen option. In role-play with children, I often find it useful for the therapist or parent to play the child's role first, to model, then have the child play it.

Externalizing Anger

While a child may be able to practice skills and solutions when calm and in session, it is another matter when the child is angry. It is, therefore, often helpful to address anger separately, head on.

The child's anger may sabotage the child's ability to moderate their behavior. I have had many children tell me that they feel they have more anger inside than anyone else in the world. While M-MAT itself should help reduce this anger, it can also be helpful to specifically externalize and address the child's anger.

First, it is important to understand the purpose and power of anger. The child's anger may have become a defender, protector, and even a friend. It gives the child a feeling of power when they would otherwise feel powerless, scared, helpless and vulnerable. It tries desperately to protect the child's sense of self. It can become addictive with its resulting adrenaline and sense of power. To act out in an angry way, to throw things and knock things over and scream and yell, in the moment, feels good. More adults would probably do so if there were not so many consequences associated with it!

The child's anger is often displaced anger. It can feel right in the moment because it is related to an earlier situation where anger was an appropriate response. For instance, a child that was verbally abused when young may be overreactive and angry in certain situations because it reminds them of the early situation and, psychologically, they are back there in that situation.

The problem with anger is that it is a trickster. Like many addictions, it can bring relief in the moment, but in the long run can cause more distress, lower self-worth, and greater life disruption.

- Externalizing Anger Role-play - One intervention that has been effective in helping children with their anger is the Externalizing Anger Role-play. It involves externalizing anger and giving the anger and the child a voice through role-play using small figures, such as sand tray figures. The process is as follows:

  Identify a situation that has brought up a lot of anger for the child (this may often come up spontaneously in the session as behavior is discussed). Briefly discuss how anger can cause problems for people, and sometimes anger is a trickster. That is, sometimes it tells us to do things that aren't good for us. Sometimes it lies to us. Ask the child to pick a figure for themself, with the direction that it has to be a positive figure. Ask the child to also pick a figure for anger. Have the child pick any other figure(s) necessary for the role-play.

For example, perhaps the child gets very angry when the child hears 'no' from a parent. The therapist can have the parent take the parent figure the child has picked out, have the child take the figure for themselves, and the therapist can take the figure for anger.

Have the parent and child start to act out the role-play with the figures:

Parent and child figures are facing each other.

Parent: "No, you can't go to Jordan's house. It is almost dinner time."

The therapist jumps in with the "Anger" figure, talking to the child figure, saying some possible cognitive distortions that anger could be saying: "That's not fair! Mom can't tell you what to do! She hates you! She never lets you do anything! Scream and yell because it's not fair!"

This externalizing of the anger and verbalizing cognitive distortions usually gives the child pause. The therapist can stop and ask the child directly, "Hmmm...Do you think what anger is saying is true?"

Anger can then jump back in and say to the child figure, "Don't listen to her! She's not your friend! I'm your only friend! You're powerful and strong with me!"

Therapist to child: "Hmmm, it sounds like anger is trying to trick you. What do you think is really true?"

Discussion and role-play can continue as appropriate. At some point, the therapist can ask the child to use the child figure to talk back to anger; to take a stand; to tell anger what is really true. The therapist can model this as well.

Through this type of role-play, using figures, the child, therapist and parent align in confronting the cognitive distortions that feed the anger.

It is important to use the figures for this intervention, as the therapist would not want to state the cognitive distortions directly to the child as there is not enough separation, and it could be counterproductive. By using the figures, everything is externalized from the child and can be observed and processed. By talking to the child as an aside, outside of the role-play, the therapist helps the child develop the more objective observer self.

The child's anger has likely been with the child for a long time and is not going to give up without a fight. This exercise, however, gives parent, child and therapist a common language in discussing anger. In subsequent sessions, the therapist can reference how anger seems to be causing problems again or inquire about a time during the week when the child was able to stand up to anger; when they could have acted out through anger but chose something different. The parent also can reference standing up to anger when they see their child starting to get angry outside of the session or notices them managing their anger well.

- Any of the many other anger management activities and games available for children can be employed to help the child learn to understand and manage their anger.

Success Focused Questions

One way to avoid focusing too much on negative behavior is by focusing on the successes or exceptions to the behavior challenges. The therapist can check in with the parent and child regularly about times the child was successful in addressing or reducing specific, identified behaviors. Below are some sample questions for both the parent and child:

> Can you think of a time that you handled anger well this week?
> Can you think of a time that your child could have lied but chose to tell the truth?
> Tell me about a time this week that Ellie got along with her sister.
> What is a time you cooperated this week?

Follow up questions may explore the why, when and how of the child's success.

The reality is that no matter how problematic a child's behavior is, there are always times when their behavior is appropriate. Exploring these times can strengthen progress and supports a new story for the child.

Givebacks

Sometimes the child has acted out in a way that is hurtful to the family, parent, or family member. Examples may be destroying property (e.g., intentionally breaking something that belongs to a parent or sibling), creating a disruption where the whole family has to change plans (e.g., acting out at an event wherein the whole family has to leave with the child) or physical aggression.

In these circumstances, the M-MAT therapist talks about "givebacks," which is a common strategy used in attachment-based parenting. Givebacks are therapeutically important for the child. The child will likely feel shame regarding the behavior, even if they appear shameless. Their own behavior has confirmed to them that they are bad, an underlying core belief. Givebacks allow the child to atone for their behavior and to be forgiven and forgive themselves so that they can move on and not continue to escalate.

In the therapy session, explain that when one person hurts or takes away from another, they have to give back to that person. The child, with the help of the parent, can brainstorm ideas for givebacks (e.g., doing sister's chores, sweeping the deck for Mom, repairing damages with dad). It is explained, however, that it is not up to the child to decide what the giveback should be. The child can give suggestions, but it is the parent, possibly with the injured party (e.g., a sibling), who gets to make the final decision on what the giveback will be, because they are the injured party. Note, however, that if the child gives reasonable suggestions, the parent is likely to get better buy-in and cooperation if they choose one of the child's suggestions.

Ideally, the therapist will have previously explained the concept of givebacks to the parent in the parent session, emphasizing the fact that following through with their child on completing the giveback often entails more work for the parent. Follow-through is important, however, as the giveback is a therapeutic intervention for the child.

No Set to Yes Set

Sometimes children are automatically oppositional. That is, they say no to just about anything their parents say. It has become habitual. Their neural pathways for a "no" response are well entrenched, while "yes" responses are rather foreign to their brain. For younger children, in particular, it can be helpful to play a game to try to increase yes responses. In this game, the therapist introduces it as a game with a great deal of excitement:

Therapist: (to child) We're going to play a game! In this game I'm going to ask you to do something, and you are going to say, "OK!" and then see how fast you can do it. So, Taylor, can you get me that ball over there? (all spoken with enthusiasm).

Child: (starts to get the ball).

Therapist: Remember, say OK (upbeat tone).

Child: OK!

Therapist: Great! Now bring me the ball! (child complies).

Therapist: Oh, good job! Now, can you jump in the air one time?

Child: OK! (child complies).

Therapist: Wonderful! Good Job! Mom, can you ask Taylor to do something?

Mom: Taylor, clap your hands two times! (with continued enthusiasm).

Child: (starts to comply).

Therapist: Say OK.

Child: OK (child complies).

Therapist and Mom: Yay! Fantastic!

Continue to alternate between the parent and the therapist giving directions to the child.

Parents are often shocked that this works, and their child is complying with requests. This intervention has been used with children up to age 7, and, to date, it has always been successful. While this, by itself, will not necessarily translate to more cooperation at home, it can be played periodically throughout the therapy and can be helpful for the habitually oppositional child.

Another good game for addressing oppositional behavior is the adaptation of "Mother May I" which can be found in Appendix A: Attachment-Based Play Activities.

Integrating Other Modalities/Therapeutic Tools

M-MAT is a complete therapeutic modality in and of itself and does not require additional tools or techniques to be effective. Nevertheless, while M-MAT is structured enough to be effective with attachment-injured children, it is also flexible enough to allow for creativity and integration of a variety of techniques and modalities in M-MAT talk.

In keeping with the multi-modal nature of M-MAT, it is completely acceptable for therapists to integrate other types of interventions into the M-MAT talk portion. As long as the therapist maintains the frame (M-MAT Play and Feeding and Questions) and starts the talk portion with the Story of Love and Attachment Narrative, while following the principles of M-MAT throughout, they can integrate other therapeutic tools while still maintaining the integrity of the M-MAT Model.

For instance, if the therapist has the requisite training, and they feel it will be helpful to the child, they can, within the structure of M-MAT, during M-MAT talk, utilize tools such as EMDR (Eye Movement Desensitization and Reprocessing), EFT (Tapping or Emotional Freedom Technique), or other useful techniques.

Conclusion

In summary, M-MAT talk is the middle part of an M-MAT session. M-MAT talk includes re-storying, skill building, psychoeducation, and addressing behavior. The story of love and the attachment narrative are always the first interventions in M-MAT talk that the therapist implements with parent and child. The talk portion of the therapy is always framed by the attachment-based play at the beginning, and the feeding and attachment questions at the end. Therapists have the flexibility in M-MAT talk to be creative and to integrate a number of therapeutic tools and interventions.

8

Working with Parents

If we value our children, we must cherish their parents.
~ John Bowlby

Parents, or other primary caregivers, are instrumental in their child's therapy and healing. Parents do not need to be perfect to be effective. They do not even need to be exceptional. They do need to have the capacity to form an attachment with their child, and be reasonably psychologically healthy, to be an instrument of change in their child's healing. Most parents can meet these criteria.

The M-MAT therapist has three major tasks in their individual work with parents. The first task is to get the parents on board with Multi-Modal Attachment Therapy (M-MAT); the second is to convey attachment-based parenting principles; and the third is to provide parent support.

Getting the Parents on Board

The first step in getting parents on board is understanding the parent's perspective. Often, the parents of attachment-injured children feel like failures. They have likely taken a child into their home to offer them a good life and a good future. They have used their parenting skills, which may have been quite effective with other children, only to find the attachment-injured child is disconnected, aggressive or passive-aggressive, angry, hurt and hurting. They may even know something about attachment and have attempted to connect with their child in an attachment oriented way, only to be rejected.

For biological parents who have changed their lives and are now ready to parent their child, guilt and shame are often strong forces to contend with. Guilt and shame can sabotage their parenting efforts. They may be too lenient in their parenting out of a sense of guilt. They may feel incapable out of a sense of shame. It is important to help these parents use their sense of guilt to help them to make changes in their parenting that are most beneficial to their child, and to let go of shame altogether.

The attachment-injured child can be a master at pulling their parents into power struggles. Parents may be unable to manage extreme behaviors and feel very out of control. The child may be disruptive to the whole family. It is not unusual to find the family's life revolving around responding to, or trying to manage, the child's behavior.

To make matters worse, everyone has an opinion on how to better parent their child. The child may be quite well behaved and even charming with others but act out in the extreme with the primary caregiver. This may lead others to believe that the parent must be doing something wrong. Parents may also have the experience of not being believed. Parents often feel isolated and blamed.

In order to gain some kind of control and order, some parents may go to more extreme parenting strategies or use harsher consequences than they would otherwise, or than they feel good about. Of course, this only makes things worse, playing into the child's mindset that they are bad and their parents are bad.

Many parents feel hopeless. Everything they have tried has failed, including other therapies. They may be trying this therapy as a last-ditch effort to save their child and their family. It is useful to give them hope, to let them know that M-MAT has helped others in their situation. It is common for parents to come to the first session expressing their commitment to their child. Then, by about the fourth or fifth session, once they are more comfortable and familiar with the therapist, and before seeing any significant change in their child, they may express that they are not sure that they can do it. They are not sure if they can parent this child. They are losing hope. Often shortly after this, the child makes their first significant shift.

A useful strategy is to ask parents to give M-MAT ten weeks total before making any decision regarding their child. By then, there should be some indication that the therapy is working. In the larger scheme of the child's and family's life, ten weeks is not very long. It can also help to discuss the process of change and that it is not likely to be linear. The child is likely to make progress gradually and will have setbacks and bad days along the way.

It is important for the therapist to listen, really listen, without judgment, to what the parents have to say. The therapist can use empathy and deep empathy to let the parents know they are heard. Parents frequently ask me if I am a parent, not because they feel I will have better information as a parent, but because they feel I will be more likely to understand and less likely to judge.

The assessment is a good time to form a therapeutic alliance with parents, as the therapist gathers information to determine the needs of the child and family. Acceptance and empathy during this process are crucial.

Once the therapist has determined, through a thorough assessment, that they are looking at a child with attachment injuries, it is time to provide psychoeducation to the parent. The therapist empathizes with the parents' struggles using deep empathy skills. The therapist can then help the parents understand attachment and the child's perspective through psychoeducation.

Information from this book can be used to educate parents or, perhaps better, parents can be referred to the book I wrote specifically for them: *Understanding Attachment Injuries in Children and How to Help: A Guide for Parents and Caregivers.* The ideas in this parent guide integrate well with M-MAT. There are, of course, other reputable authors on attachment to whom therapists can refer. Some of these can be found in Appendix B: Resources.

The therapist can let parents know that their child needs more than traditional parenting and therapy. Until the child's attachment injuries are addressed, standard parenting practices are unlikely to be effective. Often parents will feel some relief in gaining a better understanding of their child.

Something that is both important and exciting to let parents know is that they are instrumental in the healing of their child and essential to their child's therapy. Because their child was injured through relationship, much of their healing must come through relationship.

The final step in getting parents on board with M-MAT is explaining the therapy to them. Explain the process and the frame. Explain the rationale. Explain that the attachment play and feeding are regressive, and that the attachment narrative will address difficult topics. Explain that the child can choose or not choose to participate and that M-MAT uses fun and enthusiasm to engage the child. Ask the parents to allow the therapist to direct the session. Let the parents know that, during the parent/child session, they can be out of the disciplinarian role so that they can focus on the attachment with their child. Let parents know that the therapist will address any child behaviors in the session that need addressing (many parents are quite happy to be relieved of discipline duties for that period!).

Below is a summary of the steps in getting parents on board:

1. Understand the parents' perspective.
2. Communicate acceptance and empathy for parents.
3. Provide psychoeducation regarding attachment and the child's perspective.
4. Let parents know that they are instrumental in their child's healing.
5. Explain M-MAT.

Attachment-Based Parenting

I have written a whole book on attachment-based parenting: *Understanding Attachment Injuries in Children and How to Help: A Guide for Parents and Caregivers.* This book was written to help parents help their children and dovetails nicely with M-MAT. In this attachment-based parenting guide, parents will not only learn about the underlying dynamics and motivations of attachment-injured children, but also how to create safety and build connection with their child; how to help their child re-story their ideas of love, family and relationship; and, of course, practical strategies for reducing and addressing behavior. It allows parents to bring many of the M-MAT concepts into their home to support healing. Parents can truly be partners with therapists in helping their children.

There are a number of other good attachment-based parenting books available as well. I would recommend that any therapist not already familiar with attachment-based parenting do some research and find what fits for the families with whom they work. Some critical parenting areas that therapists can explore with parents include the following:

Creating Safety

Safety is the first necessary condition for any child's healing. It is the environment in which parents and children will grow and nurture the connection that will lead to emotional health. It is unlikely that any child will get better if they do not have safety. These children are already acting from an anxiety/fear attachment-injured place. When a child is in anxiety or fear, they cannot easily access the prefrontal cortex, the reasoning part of their brain. They will have difficulty processing information and making good decisions and will be unable to relax into any kind of attachment.

The therapist can brainstorm with parents strategies for increasing safety for their child by creating a safe environment, being a safe person for their child, and supporting their child in new, chaotic, or uncertain environments. Parents should be aware that even if their home is safe, their child may not feel safe due to their history. Support parents in becoming aware of their child's triggers, and attuned to their child's emotional state so they can help them when they need extra support.

Creating safety will support building attachment, and building the connection between parent and child will help the child feel safer. The two work hand in hand.

Building Connection

Building connection or attachment is the other necessary element that parents can foster in the home. Any successful parenting is based on a good relationship between parent and child, and, of course, a primary goal of M-MAT is to develop and strengthen that relationship.

Not only is attachment-based play, with the elements of touch, eye contact, mirroring and rhythm/singing, essential to the therapy, it is also useful for building and supporting the relationship in the home.

Brainstorm with parents ways they can introduce more of these elements into their home life. This may include regular structured playtimes or more spontaneous incidents of play, touch, eye contact, singing and rhythm. For instance, there is no reason a parent can't slip in a game of thumb wrestling while waiting in the doctor's office. Additionally, a parent could routinely give their child a hug in the morning or after school, come up with a special handshake, sing a goodnight song to them, use high-fives indiscriminately and/or rock their child if appropriate.

Supporting a New Story

Parents can employ several strategies to support the new story that the therapist, parent and child are creating in the therapy. This includes reading some of those great picture books mentioned previously (see appendix B), noticing positives in the moment, and focusing on, or highlighting, positive relationship experiences.

Additionally, while my recommendation is that the child's history be processed in the therapy, the therapist can coach the parents on how to respond to support the new, adaptive narrative being developed in the therapy, if the child's history comes up in conversation.

Communication

Communication is a large part of building connection and creating safety for a child. It is also instrumental in reducing and addressing behavior. How parents communicate can directly impact how children respond and how likely they are to cooperate.

Teaching parents empathy, deep empathy and other communication strategies can be very helpful. These are covered in the parenting book I wrote, but you can also find excellent parent/child communication information in the classic book: *How to Talk so Kids Will Listen and Listen so Kids Will Talk* by Adele Faber and Elaine Mazlish. These references are listed in Appendix B: Resources.

Strategies for Reducing and Addressing Behavior

The child's behavior is likely one of the reasons the parent has brought the child into therapy in the first place. They may be discovering that their usual parenting strategies aren't working. Most strategies for addressing behavior depend on a reasonably healthy parent/child attachment. As the child's attachment injuries heal, parenting will become easier.

There are attachment-based strategies to help reduce and address challenging behavior. Therapists should avail themselves of the many resources available to educate themselves, as needed, and share that information with parents. As noted, such strategies can be found in my parent guide, *Understanding Attachment Injuries in Children and How to Help: A Guide for Parents and Caregivers,* and other attachment-based parenting books.

In addition to learning parenting strategies, parents will often need help in simply staying firm, focused and consistent, and managing their own reactions to their child.

Parent Tips for Addressing Behavior Successfully

Whatever parenting strategies the therapist and parent settle on, here are some tips to help parents address behavior successfully. These address parents and are from my parenting book: *Understanding Attachment Injuries in Children and How to Help: A Guide for Parents and Caregivers.*

- **A Fresh Start** - Once your child has corrected their behavior and/or completed their redo or restore or giveback, the episode is over. Everyone needs to be able to move on. A fresh start is needed to allow your child to move towards better behavior.

- **Separate your Child from their Behavior** - Your child is going to make mistakes, and your child may even have extreme behavior. The message you want to give your child is that it is the behavior that is the problem, not your child. If a child believes they are bad, then there is not much motivation to do well, so you want to avoid shaming and blaming statements like, "bad girl" or "bad boy!" Instead, you want to talk about the behavior, "It is not OK to hit Tommy. Let's talk about what happened and how to do something different."

  Try to see your child's behavior as communication, a coping strategy, a sign of overwhelm, a way to express difficult feelings, and/or a way to gain or avoid something, rather than as a defect in your child. Though it may be counterproductive at this time, their behavior may have helped them survive at an earlier time.

  As discussed in givebacks, for hurtful behaviors, your child needs to make some kind of amends.

- **Externalize Behavior** - You can take this a step further and work on externalizing behavior. This approach comes from a type of therapy called Narrative Therapy. In externalizing behavior, you further separate the behavior from your child and then can team with your child to overcome the behavior. For instance, if your child has difficulty with temper tantrums, which we will call "throwing a fit" for the purposes of this example, you can say something like:

> Wow, that fit kind of got the better of you. You had to go to the principal's office and missed recess. Hmmm, I wonder how we could keep fits from causing you so much trouble...

Notice that it is the fit that is the problem, not the child. This opens up the space for problem solving.

Another example: Suppose your child is chronically defiant, saying "no" almost reflexively to any request. Due to defiant behavior, e.g., refusing to clean up and put their shoes on, they miss an opportunity to go sledding with their siblings and end up staying home. Your child is now sad at the missed opportunity. They say, "I wanted to go sledding!"

You sit next to them and put a hand on their shoulder. Now you could say, "Well, you should have gotten ready when I asked you!" This would be a natural response, and you wouldn't be wrong, but it is sure to evoke a defensive response from your child. Instead, you say:

> I wanted you to be able to go sledding too...Hmmm... It seems like defiance (or "a case of the no's") got in your way. It kept you from doing what you really wanted to do. I wonder how we could get defiance out of the way. It doesn't seem to be your friend...

- **Focus on how behavior causes problems for your child** - Often, parents and others try to tell a child how their behavior has caused problems for others (parents, family, peers). Until your child has developed a more secure attachment, however, they may not care. They may even be pleased to be causing others distress due to their anger and defense against their own pain, and/or the sense of power they gain from their effect upon others. So, initially, focus on how your child's behavior is causing problems for them, and try to move your child to a place of enlightened self-interest.

  In the example in the last section, with the child who had a tantrum at school, the focus is on missing recess, not that the parent was inconvenienced by the call from the school.

  As another example, if your child started screaming and yelling in the grocery store because you would not get them candy, such that you had to leave without checking out, rather than saying, "You ruined that outing for the whole family," (note that this is also NOT separating the child from the behavior) you can say, "I'm sorry that fit got in the way of getting the groceries. Now we don't have your favorite cereal. Those fits sure are pesky!"

- **Employ Calm Persistence** - Calm persistence will take you a long way in parenting. Your child will test and push for boundaries, particularly if you start doing things differently. Be the rock upon which the waves of your child's turmoil crash. Eventually, those waves will grow calmer. Your child will grow calmer when they know that you've got them; they can rely on you to be there and be consistent.

- **Don't Take Away the Things that Benefit Your Child** - If your child has something that seems to feed them as a person, where they experience success, you do not want to take that away from them as a consequence for behavior.

For instance, if your child is involved in sports, or a school club, or an art program or any other activity that they enjoy and where they are doing well, taking that away from them for unrelated behavior will almost always be counterproductive. These kinds of activities can help your child grow emotionally and socially, and give them a productive place to channel their energies. While you don't want your child overwhelmed with activities, finding one thing your child really enjoys is a blessing.

- **Don't Chase Your Child - Stay Put** - Children love to play chase! That's fine if you're playing tag in the backyard. Not so good when your child has been asked to set the table or is avoiding having that conversation about their behavior. It may be tempting to chase them, especially if your child is small and you can overtake them in two big steps, but your child will get bigger and will learn better chase strategies. Besides, that delight in their eyes as you go after them shows you how rewarding it is for them. Chasing a child is a no-win strategy for the parent.

    The exception, of course, is in a truly dangerous situation, like a child running out onto a busy street. Unless it is for safety's sake, or truly play, you don't want to chase your child.

    What you can do in those non-safety situations is to plant your feet, maybe even sit down to reinforce through body language that you are not going to chase them, then make a clear statement, calmly and firmly:

    "I'm not going to chase you."

    Followed by a direction:

"You need to come here."
"You need to set the table."

Or whatever is appropriate. If they still look like they are expecting you to chase them, repeat:

"I'm not going to chase you."

Use the broken record strategy if needed. Give them a little space to comply. If it is something that can wait, like discussing behavior, you can tell them:

"Take some time to think if you need to, and when you're ready, you need to come talk to me. No playing until you have talked to me."

- **Don't Argue with Your Child** - Arguing is one of the ways your child is able to engage you while maintaining emotional distance. As such, it may be inherently rewarding for them. Some children are expert arguers, and arguing is always a no-win situation for the parent or caregiver. Arguing gives away your power to your child.

  If you find you are arguing with your child, you can put a stop to it this way, using a calm, firm voice:

  Parent: Oh, I'm not going to argue with you!
  Child: blah blah blah blah blah....
  Parent: I'm done. I'm not arguing (spoken calmly).

Remember, it does take two to argue. Once you have clearly stated your intention, you can try to redirect your child to do something else. If that doesn't work, you can walk away, or disengage, or simply stop talking, if your child persists. Of course, you want to make sure that at other times you are providing your child with adequate time and attention. Overall the goal is to help your child begin to accept appropriate, positive attention and move away from negative attention-seeking behavior.

- **Don't Over-Lecture** - My general rule that I share with parents and caregivers is if you have explained something to your child three times, then you don't need to go into the explanation again (the exception may be if there are significant cognitive impairments). Just move on to the remind, repeat, redo, rethink, restore, or giveback as appropriate (strategies from *Understanding Attachment Injuries in Children and How to Help: A Guide for Parents and Caregivers*). Besides, if you talk at your child for a significant amount of time, they are just likely to tune you out.

- **If Your Child Lies** - Lying can be challenging to address. If it is nonsense lying, like saying the sky is green, you can simply ignore it and redirect the conversation.

    If it is an ego enhancing lie, like saying that they beat up a bully or scored all the goals in the soccer game, and you know for a fact it isn't true, you can either ignore and redirect, or respond with an empathy statement, like, "I bet sometimes you feel like beating up that bully! I can understand that, though it is important to control ourselves and not hurt others," or, "It sure would be fun to make all those goals!" If they insist that what they said is true, "I did beat him up!" or "I did score all the goals!" you can respond with, "Well, either way, I love you to the moon and back!" or "Well regardless, you are a star to me!"

    If there seems to be an argument brewing, you can say, "Hey, I'm not going to argue about it," and again redirect and/or move on.

If your child is lying about misbehavior, and you know for a fact their part in the misbehavior, you have some choices. You can ignore the lie, saying, "I know you did....so now we need to talk about making it right."

Or you can have them take some think time, "Why don't you sit at the table for a few minutes and think about what happened and your part in it. When you are ready, we'll talk about it." If they do not change their story, then move on to the above statement about making it right. Do not engage in an argument about it. If they are able to reconsider and tell a truer story, give them kudos for that shift, "Thank you for being honest with me. I appreciate it."

In either case, follow through with redo or restore or givebacks as needed.

If you are not sure what happened and the offense is not serious, but you are pretty sure they are not telling the truth, then you can say something like, "Hmmm, I think something different happened, but I'm not going to argue about it. Some day I think you will trust me enough to tell the real story."

Parent Support

All parents need support, and the saying that it takes a village to raise a child is never more true than with children struggling with attachment injuries. The therapist wants to make sure the parents have adequate support by addressing the following:

Support Network

Help parents to identify and develop their support system. The therapist can lay out the following areas and brainstorm with parents to identify and expand supports:

- Natural Supports - This includes family and friends.
- Community Supports - These are supports that are readily available in the community, such as after-school or community recreation programs.
- Schools - Does the child struggle in school? Are there school resources the family could access? Are there teachers or other school personnel who could act as an informal support for the child?
- Professional Supports - Therapists, social workers, adoption and foster agencies, public and private social service agencies may all be able to offer programs and support for children and families.
- Support Groups - Local agencies may provide support groups. Online groups are abundant. Therapists may want to screen any groups, particularly online groups, before recommending them to parents. Some groups may be filled with counterproductive attitudes or negativity.

Respite

Parents often identify respite as one of the most helpful supports for them. If the child is able to manage in various settings, this may mean having the child play at a friend's one day a week (making sure, of course, that this is a reasonably well supervised and safe situation) or attending an after-school program several days a week.

Family members or a co-parent may also be willing to spend special time with the child to give the primary caregiver a break.

If the child needs more support, some agencies may have activities geared to at-risk children or children with behavioral challenges.

Parents may feel that, due to the child's attachment injuries, they should spend all of their free time with their child. This is not true and can be counterproductive. The child needs to know that the parent can be reached and is available if a real need arises, but both parent and child can benefit from some time away.

For successful respite, it is important that the child knows when the parent is leaving and when they will return. It is important that the parent says goodbye before leaving. This may seem self-evident, but sometimes, if the child is in the habit of tantrumming when the parent leaves, and the child is at the moment engaged in some activity, it can be tempting for the parent to just slip out. This should be avoided at all costs. It will too clearly mirror early abandonment scenarios.

If time away is longer than a day, the parent should make arrangements to call in at least once a day to talk to their child. And the parent should always re-engage the child upon their reunion, including positive touch when possible.

Therapist Support

The therapist's stance with parents should always be one of support. In session, the therapist should endeavor to understand the parents' point of view and use deep empathy skills to express this understanding. The therapist should meet the parent where they are and, if needed, gently move them towards more effective parenting and useful understanding of their child. As long as they are able to develop an attachment to their child and are reasonably psychologically healthy, the parent or primary caregiver is the best chance the child has for healing and a happy life.

Outside of the session, the extent of therapist support may vary depending on the therapist and client situations. Be sure that parents have any crisis numbers that might be needed at hand, including mental health crisis, and police or sheriff, if indicated. The therapist should be sure to let parents know their crisis and callback policies, who they should contact under what circumstances, and when the therapist can be reached.

Safety Plan

If a child has unsafe behaviors, or even the likelihood of unsafe behaviors, work with parents to create a safety plan. Unsafe behavior may include violence, self-harm, dangerous impulsive behavior like running into the street, runaway behavior, and sexually acting out behavior. Ideally, a safety plan will be developed before it's needed.

Safety plans are tailored to a child's specific needs. It should include what triggers unsafe behavior, how to de-escalate the child, and what to do if parents are unable to help them de-escalate. It should include numbers to call for various levels of support, from friends or family to mental health crisis lines. The plan should clarify when to call outside resources, and all resources and contact information should be on the plan.

Therapists not familiar with safety planning should get appropriate training and supervision.

Parents should keep the safety plan readily accessible to them. Teens and older children can participate in the safety planning if they are able, and it seems appropriate.

Homework

The only homework that M-MAT requires, aside from parenting suggestions, is for parents to add touch into their relationship with their child, and to provide play and individual time for their child during the week.

What this looks like may vary depending on the child's needs and their reactivity to their parents. Discuss with the parents what might work as far as adding more touch. For one child, it may be high fives and a special handshake. For another child, it may be holding and rocking for 10 minutes before bed every night. For yet another child, it might just be a gentle hand on the shoulder now and then.

If the child is extremely reactive to the parent, adding one-on-one time may need to wait until the child is more cooperative and less reactive, as demonstrated in the therapy sessions, to increase the likelihood of positive one-on-one time for both parent and child. Of course, some children may be ready right away. Daily positive touch and once a week of one-on-one time, in addition to the therapy session, is a good goal. As the therapy moves into the last phase and towards closure, this can be increased.

It is also useful for there to be some kind of daily check-in between parent and child built into their routine. This could be part of a bedtime routine or an after-school check-in. It is a time when the parent can take a moment from their day and see how their child is doing. They can ask about their child's day, notice their child's mood, and give a hug or high five, or just a smile.

Additional homework, if it works for the parent and child, would be to practice skills at home related to skill building activities. This can help the child learn and generalize skills more quickly.

Working with Biological Parents vs. Other Caregivers

The dynamic in working with biological parents versus other caregivers can be somewhat different. With biological parents, the therapist is often dealing with the parents' sense of guilt or shame for whatever their child experienced when younger. The biological parent may be someone who is recovering from an addiction or mental illness, or who experienced domestic violence when the child was younger.

All caregivers, not just biological parents, should be screened in the initial assessment for substance use, mental illness and domestic violence concerns. The therapist wants to assure these issues have been, or are being, addressed. This may mean separate individual therapy or treatment for the parent.

Addiction and domestic violence need to be addressed before M-MAT is initiated. A parent or caregiver who is using substances cannot be the present, secure and stable person the child needs. Any violence in the home will also sabotage M-MAT. The attachment-injured child needs safety above all else to begin healing.

Biological parents may also be particularly susceptible to guilt and shame regarding their earlier parenting deficits. Help the parents distinguish between guilt and shame (guilt is feeling bad for their mistakes and how they might have hurt their child, shame is the sense that they are bad and bad parents). Help them to let go of the shame, and use the guilt constructively to do something different now.

Guilt can sometimes lead to overly permissive parenting, which is not what any child needs, much less an attachment-injured child. The therapist works to help the parent see that what their child needs is firm and consistent parenting.

The attachment-injured child may also use the parent's sense of guilt or shame to try and get a reaction from them.

Work with the parent specifically on these triggers and how to respond.

Biological parents are also more likely to be triggered in the telling of the child's attachment narrative. Their child's story is also their story. Be sure that the parent understands what the attachment narrative involves. If parents become emotional in the parent/child session, proceed as described in chapter 7: M-MAT Talk to help the child understand that the parent is OK and have a sense of containment.

With caregivers who are not the biological parents, there is a greater chance of the child losing the placement and connection forever, particularly for non-relative placements. If the caregiver sincerely wants to parent the child but is struggling because of the child's behavior, they are a perfect candidate for M-MAT. In these circumstances, offer hope to the caregivers and ask them to engage in M-MAT for at least ten weeks before making any decision, stating that there should be at least some shift in that period, enough to give hope to the parent/caregiver to continue the therapy.

If the caregiver never really wanted the child, or is not attached or able to attach, then the therapist may quickly find they need to move to M-MAT Individual. Sometimes the parent is upfront with expressions of a lack of attachment, and sometimes not. Sometimes the parent may demonstrate their lack of readiness by simply not showing up and/or missing multiple appointments.

If the parent is sincere in wanting to connect with their child, but their own attachment issues are getting in the way, individual therapy for the parent may be indicated. Be careful, however, not to mistake hopelessness, frustration and fatigue as a lack of commitment or attachment on the caregiver's part. If it is a viable home and attachment for the child, all efforts should be made to preserve the placement.

Conclusion

The best chance an attachment-injured child has for a happy, healthy life is to develop a positive attachment to their primary caregiver. This forms a solid base for the child's development. Therefore, the parent is crucial in the child's therapy. The M-MAT therapist can help parents help their child by providing psychoeducation regarding attachment theory and the attachment-injured child; explaining and encouraging engagement in M-MAT; providing attachment-based parenting education; and working with the parents on their support system.

9

Putting It All Together

Below are a few notes on putting all of the Multi-Modal Attachment Therapy (M-MAT) pieces together to create a successful therapy for child and parent.

Adjusting for the Child's Age

Five to 12 years is a wide age range in child development terms. And, M-MAT has been successfully used with children 4 to 16 years of age, an even wider age range.

When working with children, the therapist should adjust the work according to the child's developmental and emotional age. Generally speaking, with younger children, the session will involve more play and less talk. Older children are more likely to be able to contribute significantly to the attachment narrative than younger children. This is not always the case, however. An extremely bright and insightful 5-year-old may contribute significantly to the talk portion of M-MAT, while a much older child may be initially mute in the sessions. Remember, though, that in the therapy, the parent and therapist are responsible for providing the play opportunities and re-storying for the child.

Attachment-injured children can be pseudo-mature, acting in some ways older than their age and eschewing "baby" things. The therapist should take care not to let this fool them and make the mistake of shying away from attachment play with these children. When the therapist describes M-MAT to parents, they may state that they do not believe their child will want to participate in the attachment-based play because it is too babyish. To date, I have not found a child who has not ultimately relished this play. Usually, the child takes to it right away because it fills such an important, unmet need within them.

Ultimately, use common sense. There may be more holding and rocking with younger children than older. Yet, for an older child who missed out on rocking and holding, it may be an important intervention for their healing. Evaluate each child and family's needs individually. Gauge the child's response. Remember that M-MAT attachment play is by its nature regressive because M-MAT is attempting to heal the younger injured child within any child, so do not be afraid to go young in the play. The complexity of the activities can be tailored to the child's developmental level. For instance, for a developmentally young child, the therapist may play a patty-cake clapping game with parent and child. For an older child, the therapist may choose to play any of the many more complicated clapping games.

Working with Teens

M-MAT has been successfully implemented with teens up to age 16 and their parents. Teens are, and should be, more autonomous than younger children. They are in a different developmental stage with a stronger need for differentiation from their parents. If they do not have a solid attachment base, however, they will struggle with this developmental task. They may be inappropriately clingy, or very hostile, or very disengaged from their parents. Underlying all this, exists an injured child.

In working with teens, begin sessions with more limited attachment-based play, choosing older activities such as clapping games and hand stack or mirrors. The therapist may choose to do only one or two play activities each session. Begin the talk portion with the Story of Love and move to the Attachment Narrative. The Attachment Narrative is well suited to teens. At this age, they are able to contribute quite a bit to their story with the parent filling in the gaps, and parent and therapist supporting cognitive corrections and highlighting a helpful and adaptive story of the teen's life.

For teens, the attachment narrative usually takes longer than for younger children, both because they have had a longer life and because the teen is able to contribute much more to the conversation. The therapist can take time with the narrative. Teens are usually very interested in the telling of their story. The attachment narrative can be a very powerful tool in working with teens and their parents, and it is not unusual for previously undisclosed trauma to surface when working with teens and parents on the attachment narrative.

As with younger children, once the attachment narrative is complete, the therapy can then move on to other talk topics such as skill building and behavior.

The session is ended with a snack and attachment questions. Whether the parent actually feeds the teen depends on the needs and responses of the teen. Still, the snack is provided as each question is answered. Relationship questions are used. With teens, the therapist may choose to add some questions that target things the teen and parent are specifically working on, focusing on successes. Regardless, appreciations and fun continue to be emphasized (see chapter 6: M-MAT Feeding and Questions). Thus, the frame is maintained, and the parent and youth end on a positive note.

Therapy Timeline

The therapy timeline will vary from child to child, but a sample timeline for parent/child sessions may look like this:

Session 1:

- Attachment-Based Play
- Story of Love
- Feeding and Questions

Sessions 2-4

- Attachment-Based Play
- Attachment Narrative
- Feeding and Questions

Session 5

- Attachment-Based Play
- Self-Soothing Skills
- Feeding and Questions

Session 6

- Attachment-Based Play
- Communication Skills
- Feeding and Questions

Session 7

- Attachment-Based Play
- What Babies Need
- Feeding and Questions

Session 8

- Attachment-Based Play
- Feeling Identification Skills, Self-Soothing Skills (remember, repetition is good)
- Feeding and Questions

Session 9

- Attachment-Based Play
- Addressing Behavior, Self-Soothing Skills
- Feeding and Questions

Session 10

- Attachment-based Play
- Parent/Child Roles
- Feeding and Questions

Session 11...

- Attachment-Based Play
- (Skill Building, Addressing Behaviors, Re-storying, and Psychoeducation, repeating as needed)
- Feeding and Questions

Note that in all sessions, the frame of attachment-based play and feeding and questions is utilized. Once the Story of Love and Attachment Narrative have been completed, the talk portion of the session can move to skill building, psychoeducation and addressing behavior, as needed. Exactly which activity should be planned for each session should be determined by the most pressing needs presented by the child. In general, self-soothing skills should be worked on early in the therapy.

There may be times when returning to the attachment narrative is necessary to fill in missing pieces, to reference when exploring and striving to understand current behavior, or when pieces of the child's history come up for the child.

Each session should be planned beforehand. This means having a list of attachment-based play activities and attachment questions for the session, along with a plan for the talk portion. This will help keep the therapy on track. Of course, the therapist may sometimes need to adjust a session at the time, based on immediate needs. The therapist needs to be careful, however, to not end up responding each week to a new 'Crisis of the Week,' which can sabotage moving forward in the therapy. In any case, the frame (attachment-based play, and feeding and questions) should always be maintained if at all possible. If the child refuses to cooperate, that is OK. The therapist can engage in these with the parents. The therapist can adjust the play and talk sections, shortening or lengthening each as needed, to address immediate concerns. The frame, however, should still be maintained.

After each session, the therapist can reflect on the session in planning the next session.

Summary of M-MAT Talk Topics and Interventions

Below are summaries of topics and interventions for the four areas of M-MAT Talk (Re-Storying, Skill Building, Psychoeducation, and Addressing Behavior) for ease of planning sessions.

Summary of Re-Storying interventions:

- Story of Love
- Attachment Narrative
- What Do Babies Need?
- Storytime
- Heart of Hearts

Summary of Skill Building and Psychoeducation topics:

- Self-Regulation/Self-Soothing
- Feeling Identification and Expression
- Communication Skills
- Boundaries
- Problem Solving
- Social Skills
- Shame vs. Healthy Guilt
- Parent/Child Roles
- Clarifying Responsibility

Summary of Addressing Behavior interventions:

- Discussion
- Problem Solving
- Externalizing Anger
- Success Focused Questions
- Givebacks
- No Set to Yes Set

Sample Session Plan

Always have the session planned ahead of time. Both the play and talk sections should be planned. The therapist should also have the snack planned, and, if they are new to M-MAT, it can be helpful to have the attachment questions used with the snack written out as well. It is useful to bring to session a list of the attachment-based play activities that the therapist has decided to use for that session. A sample session plan may look like this:

PLAY
- Double Double (clapping game) (touch and rhythm)
- Fast Slow Clapping (mirroring)
- Breathe Together (touch, mirroring, rhythm)
- Row Row Row Your Boat (eye contact, touch, rhythm)
- Gentle Touch (touch)

TALK
- Continue Attachment Narrative

FEEDING AND QUESTIONS
- A time Mom had fun with her child
- A time the child had fun with Mom
- Something Mom did for her child this week

- Something the child did for their mom or family this week
- Something each looks forward to doing together in the future

A reminder that repetition of activities and questions is good and desirable across sessions throughout the therapy.

10

M-MAT Individual

M-MAT Individual is an adaptation of the regular M-MAT model for children who do not have an adult committed to them and/or available to participate in therapy.

Rationale

There are, unfortunately, many children who do not have an adult available for the long term. Therapists may work with these children in shelters for abused and neglected children, foster family agencies, treatment programs and other similar settings. Therapists may also find themselves working with a child who is living with a permanent caregiver who is either unwilling or unable to attach to the child or commit to the therapy. Children with attachment injuries who have no committed adult are at great risk for life difficulties.

Multi-Modal Attachment Therapy Individual (M-MAT Individual) is designed for working with children with significant attachment injuries who have no appropriate, committed, long-term caregiver; and who will be able to participate with the therapist at least weekly for at least 4 or 5 months. The target age of 5 to 12 years of age is the same as for M-MAT. As always, the therapist should start with a full assessment of the child to determine the child's needs.

The goal of M-MAT Individual, as in M-MAT, is still to help attachment-injured children develop a template for positive relationships and the inner resources necessary to be successful in life. How is that achieved without a caregiver to work with? In the case of M-MAT Individual, the therapist engages in the attachment-based play with the child to provide the needed touch, eye contact, mirroring and rhythm, to facilitate healing. It is important to note that the therapist is in no way trying to take on the parenting role. The therapist must always be aware of, and maintain, therapeutic boundaries. How to maintain boundaries while doing this work is described further in this chapter.

Some people may question the wisdom of engaging in attachment-based play with the child, when the therapist is likely short term in the child's life. This is a legitimate concern, and below are strategies to minimize emotional distress for the child. The M-MAT attachment-based play elements of safe touch, eye contact, mirroring and rhythm are desperately needed by the child and, when provided with appropriate boundaries, are healing in and of themselves.

There is the possibility that the child will develop an attachment to the therapist, and this is OK, and even a sign of health. Consider that the child with no template at all for relationship is at far more risk than the child with at least one experience, one positive template. Once the child has internalized one positive relationship with an adult, the child will have a better chance of being successful in future relationships and, therefore, in life in general.

M-MAT Individual Overview

M-MAT Individual is similar to M-MAT in many ways and is based on the same principles and concepts. To understand M-MAT Individual, first understand M-MAT as described in this book.

Similar to M-MAT, M-MAT Individual is a structured therapy employing both play and talk portions with the goals of healing relationship, developing a positive narrative and building skills.

Differences, which will be discussed below, include boundaries, structure, transferring attachment, and closure.

Therapeutic Boundaries

While many of the principles for M-MAT Individual and M-MAT are the same, working with an attachment-injured child individually is very different from working with a parent in the room. When the M-MAT therapist is working with parent and child, the therapist strives to support attachment and closeness between the parent and child. The parent/child relationship, however, is quite different from the therapist/child relationship. The therapist is a relative stranger to the child and is likely in the child's life for a limited amount of time. The boundaries between parent and child, and therapist and child, therefore, are different. While the M-MAT therapist may encourage a child to climb into their parent's lap, the therapist would set appropriate boundaries if a latency age child tried to climb into their lap.

The therapist can help set boundaries and expectations by identifying themself as a "helper person" in the child's life. This can be done at the first meeting. The therapist can say something like, "I have a cool job. My only job is to help you! I don't get kids in trouble; I only try to help them. I can be a helper person in your life." If the child is in a temporary setting where the therapist is working, the therapist can further say, "While you are here, I will be one of your helper people." This sets a time frame and can later be used to distinguish between helper people and forever people in the child's life.

If the child has difficulty with boundaries, teach specifically to this, both in the moment and during the talk portion of the session. For instance, if a child the therapist just met indiscriminately jumps into their lap, the therapist can gently move them to the seat next to them and say something like, "Oh, let me shake your hand! I don't know you very well, and you don't know me very well, so we should shake hands. You only want to sit in the lap of people you know very well!" The therapist can then plan to teach to appropriate boundaries in the skill building part of talk therapy at a later time.

Session Structure

The M-MAT Individual sessions are structured similarly to the M-MAT parent/child sessions. There is a beginning, a middle and an end, with attachment-based play at the beginning, and questions at the end, framing the middle portion. The purpose of the structure is the same as for M-MAT in that it creates consistency and safety and is therapeutic in and of itself.

One of the differences in individual therapy is the inclusion of a non-directive play portion, which occurs after the talk portion. It is useful to say, "First we will play my games, then we will play what you want to play!" If the therapist works in a play therapy room with toys, the child will likely be drawn to the toys. This provides motivation for the child and allows the child to further process through play, while still allowing the attachment work. The session structure, with approximate times for a 50 minute session, is as follows:

1. Attachment-Based Play: The Frame Part 1 (5 minutes)
2. M-MAT Talk (20 minutes)
3. Non-Directive Play (20 minutes)
4. Success Questions: The Frame Part 2 (5 minutes)

Of course, the timing of each of the sections depends on what works for any given child. In general, a younger child will involve more play and less talk.

How each of these M-MAT Individual components is the same as or different from those in M-MAT is described below. Please read the earlier portions of the book to understand the components fully.

M-MAT Individual Play

The implementation of attachment-based play between therapist and child is probably the component that most differentiates M-MAT Individual from other individual child therapies. The attachment-based play is the first part of the session and, along with the success questions, frames the middle talk and non-directive play sections.

The therapist engages in attachment-based play with the child and helps maintain boundaries by choosing less intimate, less threatening attachment-based play activities. Appropriate activities include clapping games, high fives, thumb wrestling, follow the leader games, and eye contact games (e.g., staring contests). One way to gauge this is to think about what activities would be appropriate peer to peer. These activities would likely be appropriate for the therapist and child. The therapist avoids activities such as gentle touch and holding/rocking activities. Also, as always, the child always has permission not to participate. In Appendix A: Attachment-Based Play Activities, activities appropriate for individual therapy are identified with the letter "I".

There is no need to encourage touch outside of the attachment play. The therapist does not initiate hugs. If the child is overly physical, the therapist can use it as an opportunity to teach boundaries. If necessary, the therapist can teach a side hug, wherein the parties hug with one arm from the side, around the shoulders, for a count of three. The therapist can also substitute high fives or handshakes for hugs. Some children will avoid touch altogether outside of the attachment-based play which is fine, and appropriate.

Though less intimate, the touch, mirroring, eye contact and rhythm in M-MAT Individual attachment-based play is still healing for the child.

M-MAT Individual Talk

M-MAT Individual Talk is the second part of the session and occurs directly following the attachment-based play. As in M-MAT, the talk portion of M-MAT Individual includes re-storying, skill building, psychoeducation and addressing behavior.

Re-Storying

In M-MAT Individual, re-storying does not include the story of love, as that requires a parent. The attachment narrative also requires a caregiver in the room, so there is no pressure on the child, and the child can just listen to the conversation, if that is their wont. The child may not be able to tolerate well a direct conversation with the therapist about their history, and, without a permanent, committed caregiver, the child does not have a secure base to support them.

The therapist can, however, address the child's history. The therapist should review the child's history outside the session to understand the themes of the child's story. The therapist can then plan out sessions to address those themes using story/metaphor and psychoeducation. For example, if the child was exposed to domestic violence, the therapist can tell the story of April the rabbit, who lived in a rabbit hole where there was fighting all the time! In the story, the therapist wants to address empathy for the child (or character in the story), fault and responsibility, and possibly apology.

In a subsequent session, the therapist may provide direct psychoeducation about how children sometimes feel when the grownups around them fight and why it is never the child's fault. The psychoeducation is provided without expecting anything from the child, allowing the child to play or draw if they wish while the therapist talks.

The therapist can also read to the child any of the many children's books that address themes with which the child may be struggling.

Because the therapist is a stranger to the child, addressing the child's history may come a little later in the course of individual therapy, after the therapist has developed some rapport with the child, and the child is demonstrating some comfort in the session with the therapist.

One way to create a new story in the absence of a caregiver is to explore with the child if they ever had someone, anyone, (a teacher, relative, friend, etc.) in their life who was supportive. You can explore this with questions that expand on this and reflect a positive image of themself back to them. This helps re-story their ideas about relationships and self. Some good questions along these lines include:

> Is there anyone who you felt really saw who you were?
> Who saw the good in you?
> What did they see in you?
> I wonder what they would tell me about you.
> If I asked them what was special about you, I'm curious what they would say.
> I'm wondering if there is someone in your life who you felt really cared about you.
> How did they show they cared? How could you tell?
> Is there anyone who helped you out when you needed help?
> How did they help you?
> Why do you think they helped you?

Use reflection and highlighting to emphasize positive responses.

Some of these questions will be better with older children than younger ones. For younger children, the therapist can help supply answers if needed (e.g., Do you think they saw how smart (kind, funny, etc.) you are?). Sometimes a child will identify a pet. That is fine. The same questions apply.

If a child brings up a challenging or traumatic experience from their past, the therapist can help the child process the experience, explore feelings, provide empathy and address the themes of fault and responsibility and provide psychoeducation as needed, covering the same themes they would in the attachment narrative. Additionally, if appropriate to the situation, the therapist can offer an apology to the child as they might have had the parent do. This may look like this:

I am so sorry that happened to you. If I could, I would have (the perpetrator) get down on their knees and apologize to you. No adult should treat a child that way. As an adult, representing adults, I want to apologize to you that you were hurt like that. I am so sorry. You didn't deserve that. You deserve to be treated kindly and well cared for.

Skill Building

Skill building is the same in M-MAT Individual as in M-MAT and includes self-regulation/self-soothing; feelings identification and expression; communication skills; boundaries; and problem solving and social skills as needed.

Psychoeducation

Psychoeducation regarding shame and guilt and clarifying responsibility is equally as relevant in M-MAT Individual as it is in M-MAT. Psychoeducation regarding parent/child roles may come up in relation to the child's current living situation or history and should be discussed as needed.

Addressing Behavior

Behavior outside the session is addressed as needed. Whatever the child's living situation, they may be displaying behavior that is causing them a great deal of difficulty and maybe even threatening their placement. Use acceptance and empathy to team with the child in assessing what is occurring and how to be more successful. Externalizing anger and the behavior, and CBT (Cognitive Behavioral Therapy) role-play, as discussed in chapter 7: M-MAT Talk, can be useful in achieving these goals.

M-MAT Individual Non-Directive Play

The third part of the session is non-directive play. M-MAT Individual differs from M-MAT in that it includes non-directive play in the session. Note that while M-MAT Individual uses non-directive play, it is not the same as Non-Directive Play Therapy. Non-Directive Play Therapy has its own set of protocols and principles which are often quite different from M-MAT Individual.

While Non-Directive Play Therapy, as previously discussed, is insufficient for treating children with attachment injuries, non-directive or child-centered play, when integrated into M-MAT Individual, appears to be helpful. The non-directive play occurs after the talk portion and before the closing questions. It gives the child the space to integrate the information from the talk portion and process in a different manner. It also provides some relief from the more intense interactional part of the therapy.

As in traditional non-directive play, the therapist can provide reflective comments. For M-MAT Individual, it is not necessary for the child to engage in imaginative play activities. It is fine if the child wants to play a board game with the therapist, or read, or build with blocks. The child and therapist enjoying this time together in a way that is not pressured or goal-oriented supports an appropriate attachment and also allows the child to get grounded and ready to re-enter the world.

M-MAT Individual Success Questions

In M-MAT Individual, the therapist includes the frame for the session, with attachment play at the beginning and success questions at the end, but eliminates the feeding portion, as feeding the child is more aligned with parental boundaries.

The questions, also, are not focused on relationship in the same way as they are with the parent in M-MAT. They are success oriented questions rather than attachment oriented. So, for instance, in M-MAT, the therapist may ask a child about a time they had fun with their parent. In M-MAT Individual, the therapist may simply ask about a time they had fun or a positive experience they had that day. Or the therapist and child may engage in a closing ritual of saying three good things that happened that week or three good things about themselves. The therapist can also focus questions on successes the child is experiencing on therapy goals. Thus, the closing questions for M-MAT Individual are positive and success oriented but less relational. Hence, the closing questions in M-MAT Individual are referred to as success questions, rather than attachment questions as in M-MAT.

Though less relational, the success questions still serve to create a new, success oriented storyline or narrative for the child.

Some examples:

A time this week you had fun.
A time this week you smiled.
A time this week you stood up to anger.
A time this week you told the truth (or whatever their goals may be).
Something you appreciate about yourself.
Something you did for someone.
Something someone else did for you.
Three good things about yourself.
Something you are proud of.
Something you accomplished this week (or day, month).
Qualities you appreciate about yourself.

Transferring Attachment

If the child is moving to a permanent placement, then M-MAT with the child and new caregiver would be an ideal continuation of the therapy. In many circumstances, however, the therapist will not be continuing with the child in their new placement. If the child and caregiver can be referred to another therapist for M-MAT, that would be the next best option.

If the therapist will no longer be working with the child, the therapist will want to provide several sessions with the child and caregiver during the transition, if possible. The therapist should endeavor to talk with the caregiver first to understand their commitment to the child and explain that the purpose of the transition sessions is to support the connection of the child and caregiver and the transition to the new home.

In the caregiver/child sessions, the M-MAT structure is maintained with the frame and talk portions. The talk portion, however, focuses on the transition and the new relationship. The therapist can encourage discussion of the positive reasons the caregiver is taking the child into their home. The therapist can help the child express any concerns, questions and worries they might have. The therapist can explore with the child and new caregiver their hopes and wishes for the future and each other. If they are not familiar with each other, the session can include getting-to-know-you questions and activities.

In the attachment-based play portion, the therapist can support the connection between the child and caregiver through the play. If the new caregiver is not well known to the child, then the play should be appropriate to the level of unfamiliarity, similar to the guidelines for child/therapist play, and the therapist should participate as well.

Appropriate boundaries should be maintained, and the child should not feel forced to participate. The goal should be to have some fun to support the new relationship, and, as always, the child's boundaries should be respected.

If there has not been a feeding/snack portion in the individual session, then it should not be introduced this late in the therapy unless the therapist will be continuing with this child and caregiver. In the ending questions, if the caregiver and child have enough history together, the therapist can introduce positive attachment questions, such as a time they had fun together. They can also introduce questions about experiences the child and caregiver would like to have together in the future.

Closure

Not all children will develop a strong attachment to the therapist during M-MAT Individual, but some may. Given that the child has attachment injuries and may have developed some attachment to their therapist, it is particularly important how the therapist handles closure. Consistent with M-MAT principles, the therapist wants to pay particular attention to shaping the meaning the child makes of the closure. The child needs to walk away feeling that they are valued. This can be done in several ways.

One way is to use the last session with the child to honor the child and the relationship. This may include bringing a special snack or treat and setting up a special activity. Creating cards for each other is a nice closing activity, with the therapist supplying a variety of materials, including glitter, stickers and markers. The cards are then given to each other during the session. It provides an opportunity for the therapist to write special things about the child in the card. The card can become a transition object that the child takes with them.

It is also very good to provide an additional transition object for the child. While gift giving during the course of therapy is counterproductive, a special little gift, such as a special stone or other object, given during the last session, can serve as an additional transition object. One strategy for reducing the potential for distress at the possible loss of the object is to tell the child that the object represents the child's specialness and good wishes for them, and, even if someday they lose or misplace the object, it will not matter because the specialness and good wishes will still be there.

The child can also be acknowledged for any progress and successes they have made. In some instances, the closure could be likened to a successful graduation.

The therapist should be talking to the child at least a few weeks before closure about the ending of the therapy. One way for the therapist to validate the child and make positive meaning is for the therapist to share both their feelings at the ending, and also their excitement for the child's future. The therapist needs to be genuine and age-appropriate for the child. This may look something like this:

> I am really going to miss you! I have enjoyed our time together and getting to know you. I am very excited and happy for you, though, because I know you are going to a home where you will get the care that you need and deserve!

For older children, if the therapist feels that the child has developed a healthy, positive attachment, they can use this as a reference point for the child saying something like:

> I feel like we have developed a good relationship. I feel like we respect and care about each other. This is

good because now you know what this feels like to be in a good relationship. Although all relationships are different, you'll be able to know if a relationship feels like a good relationship.

The child may ask questions like, "Why can't I live with you?" or, "Can you adopt me?" This may be a sign of a genuine attachment or indiscriminate attachment. Regardless, the answer can be the same. After validating the child's feelings, the answer needs to focus on the therapist's limitations and that the child deserves more. A possible response:

> You would like to come home with me. I appreciate that! I sure have enjoyed our time together, and I will miss you. I'm afraid that I am only a helper person in your life, though. I'm not able to be there for you all the time. You deserve a forever home and someone who can be there for you all the time (if this is the plan for the child). You need and deserve more than I can give you.

It is also important to acknowledge and validate underlying feelings and how hard goodbyes can be.

Appendix A: Attachment-Based Play Activities

Almost any playful activity that includes touch, eye contact, mirroring and/or rhythm will work for M-MAT play. Most games played with very young children will work. Avoid competitive and intellectual games or activities. Be creative, but make sure the activity includes at least one of the critical elements: Touch, Eye Contact, Mirroring, Rhythm.

The relevant elements of each activity in this appendix are indicated by a letter following the description as so:

T: Touch; E: Eye Contact; M: Mirroring; R: Rhythm

Activities that are suitable for M-MAT Individual (Multi-Modal Attachment Therapy - Individual) are indicated with an (I)

The following activities have been collected from multiple sources. For M-MAT, all attachment-based play must include Touch, Eye Contact, Mirroring and/or Rhythm. Any activities found online or through other sources should be evaluated for these elements before integrating into an M-

MAT session. Other programs or sources, including Theraplay®, may have different criteria for attachment-based play, and some activities may not meet the requirement for M-MAT play.

Most activities selected for a session should be repeated several times within the session before moving on to the next activity. If the client and family have gained mastery in the activity, some activities, such as clapping games, can be altered to increase complexity or to go faster or slower, to add variety and challenge as needed. The activities below are listed in alphabetical order.

All Around the Garden
Adult traces a circle on child's hand singing:
"All around the garden like a little mouse"
Then walks their fingers up the child's arm singing:
"One step, two step"
Then runs their fingers up the arm for a gentle tickle under the chin with:
"In your little house"
(T R)

Baby Powder Hand or Foot Prints
Lightly powder the child's hands or feet and make prints on black or dark paper. (T) (I)

Blindfold Touch Walk
Child is blindfolded. Therapist stands on one side with their hands on the child's wrist and arm, and parent is on the other with a hand on the child's wrist and arm. Parent and therapist walk with the child around the room. Therapist and parent take turns having the child touch different objects and child guesses what they are touching. I always have the child eventually touch the parent's hair or skin and guess. If appropriate (child is old enough/safe enough),

parent and child can change places. This activity requires a level of trust and is usually better a little later in the therapy process. (T)

Body Part Sounds
This one can be good for the reluctant child. The therapist or parent might discover that when they touch the child's foot, it makes a "ring-a-ling" sound, and when they touch their nose, it "beeps", etc. (T)

Breathe Together
Therapist, parent and child hold hands. Therapist leads and as they raise their hands, they breathe in, and as they lower their hands, they breathe out. Therapist can coach "nice deep breaths". (T M R) (I)

Clapping Games
Patty Cake, Double Double, or any other child clapping game will work. In these games, you have both non-threatening touch and mirroring occurring. This can be done three ways with parent, child and therapist clapping together; or just between parent and child. You can find any number of clapping games online. (T M R) (I)

Clap Patterns
Therapist starts by clapping a pattern. The parent and child repeat the pattern simultaneously in a call/response pattern. After therapist takes a few turns, the parent leads the clapping, then the child. (T M R) (I)

Comparing Body Parts
A very simple activity in which the parent and child compare the size or other aspects of body parts. For instance, putting hands up against each other's and seeing how big/small each is, or seeing how high child's head reaches on parents' body,

etc. They can also compare color, shape, freckles, etc. Can also introduce past and future orientation by saying things like, "Can you remember when your child's hand was even smaller than this?" or "I bet he may grow up to be even taller than you someday." (T M)

Eye Blink Pattern

Have the child look at the adult in the eye while the adult blinks a pattern (e.g., blink pause blink blink). The child then blinks the pattern back to the adult. The child can then have a turn to initiate the pattern. Very young children may find this too difficult. (E M) (I)

Eye Color Guess

Therapist tells parent and child, "Close your eyes and don't look!"
Then, "Now, without looking, Mom, can you tell me what color (child's) eyes are?"
"(To child) can you tell me what color your mom's eyes are?"
"OK, now open your eyes and take a look and see if you are right!"
Parent and child now look at each other's eyes.
"Can you see any other colors?"
This is a one time activity, often done early in the course of therapy, that encourages non-threatening eye contact. (E)

Fast/Slow Clapping

The leader starts clapping at a steady pace, and others clap with the leader. The leader then varies the pace of the clapping, faster and slower, while the others follow. Participants take turns being the leader. (M R)

Feeling Faces

One person makes a face depicting an emotion while looking at the other person. The other person copies that face and guesses the emotion. This can also be done in a group where the face is passed around the group. It is then the next person's turn. (E M) (I)

Follow the Leader

This can be done moving around the room in different ways. Or it may be more appropriate to do this sitting down where you move your hands (e.g., clapping, patting your thighs, etc.) and possibly head in a rhythmic pattern. I usually make changes on counts of four or multiples of four, making it easier to follow. The child can have a turn to be leader after the adults. (M R) (I)

Gentle Touch

A very simple activity to be used with children of all ages. I have at times used it every session as a closing to the play part of the session. Parent touches the child appropriately, gently, and child touches the parent back in the same way. It is then the child's turn to touch the parent in some appropriate way, and the parent touches back in the same way. Repeat several times. This is one that the therapist usually stays out of. (T M)

Hand Squeeze Message

All participants hold hands in a circle. The first person squeezes the hand of a person next to them in some kind of pattern such as "squeeze squeeze pause squeeze squeeze". That person passes the squeeze pattern on to the next person in the group, and it goes around the circle back to the first person who says if it comes back the same as it went out. I often instruct participants to close their eyes, or at least not watch the squeezing as it goes around the circle. I also instruct them to keep the pattern simple, usually no more than 5 to 7 squeezes, depending on the age/ability of the group. Note that the group may be just the parent, child and therapist. (T) (I)

Hand Squeeze Pattern
Adult and child face each other holding hands. Adult starts and squeezes a pattern, e.g., left, left, right, right. Child squeezes back the same pattern. Participants can be instructed to maintain eye contact throughout, if desired. Then it is the child's turn. (T E M) (I)

Hand Stack
Each person puts a hand in the stack and then their other hand, in the same order, so all the hands are stacked up. Then the person with their hand on the top moves it to the bottom, the next person does the same, etc. Start out slow. At some point, you can reverse the order, and the hand on the bottom moves to the top of the stack. Usually, this game picks up speed until there is fun chaos. (T) (I)

Itsy Bitsy Spider
Sing the classic song, but facilitate parent and child doing movements together, i.e., each uses a hand, and they work together to do the movement for the 'spider' moving up the water spout. This is tricky. Better for a little older child.
(T R)

Mirrors
Child and parent, or therapist, face each other. First, the adult moves slowly and the child follows, then the child leads. I instruct parent and child to look in each other's eyes the whole time and see if they can move together so that I cannot tell who is leading and who is following. For older clients, the parent and child can pick who is going to lead without the therapist knowing, and then see if the therapist can guess who the leader is. This can be done either

standing, or sitting just using hands and head movements. (E M) (I)

Mother May I
Played the usual way, but directions include things like, "hug your child and take one step forward" or "move up to where your mother is and give her a high five". If the child is sent back to start, I invariably give direction to parent, "go back to start, take your child's hand, and bring him X number of steps forward". Complexity of directions depends on the age and ability of the child. I always have them reach me at the same time. Parent then gets a turn to direct. In this game, I never give the child a turn to direct, saying they are too young to be the "mother," thus maintaining the hierarchy. (T)

Motorboat, Motorboat
Participants stand in a circle holding hands. They move slowly in a circle singing, "motorboat, motorboat go so slow," they then pick up speed singing, "motorboat, motorboat go so fast," and finally, go even faster with "motorboat, motorboat step on the gas" until therapist or parent calls "stop" and they freeze, then do the same thing in the opposite direction. (T R) (I)

Peanut Butter – Jelly
One person says, "peanut butter," the others reply with "jelly" mimicking the same intonation/speed etc. They do this a number of times, changing tone, pitch, volume and speed (e.g., whispering slowly, or using a high, squeaky voice). (M R) (I)

Peek-A-Boo
Classic peek-a-boo. This is a good one to use when the child is shy and hiding their eyes. The adult can engage the child

with a playful, "Where is _____. There they are!" as the adult discovers the child. They can then allow the child to hide again and repeat. If the child is strongly withdrawing, the adult can give the child additional blankets, etc., to hide behind, thus going with, rather than against, the resistance, and maybe at first only discovering a foot or elbow. (E) (I)

Ring Around the Rosie (almost)
All participants hold hands in a circle and move clockwise or counterclockwise while singing the traditional "Ring around the Rosie" song, BUT at the end, instead of "we all fall down," whoever is 'it' calls out a movement, such as "we all clap our hands" or "we all stamp our feet" and the participants engage in that movement. It is then the next person's turn. (T M R) (I)

Rock-A-Bye-Baby (almost)
Parent holds or rocks child in whatever way is appropriate and comfortable while parent and therapist sing traditional "Rock-a-bye-baby" song, BUT, replace the word "baby" with the child's name, and at the end, instead of "down will come baby, cradle and all" sing, "and we will catch _child's name_ cradle and all." The therapist can direct parent and child to look at each other's eyes throughout the song, and repeat as appropriate. (T E R)

Row, Row, Row Your Boat (almost)
Child stands or sits between parent and therapist. Parent and therapist hold hands, making the 'boat'. Child puts their hands on the adults' hands as they row the boat to the song. Have the child facing the parent and ask them if they can look into their parent's eyes the whole time, singing the song:

Row, row, row your boat gently down the stream,
Merrily, merrily, merrily, merrily <u>child's name</u> is such a dream!
Repeat as you want. (T E R)

Run to Mom (or Dad)

The therapist sits in a chair opposite parent. The child stands in front of the therapist, facing away from the therapist and towards the parent. The therapist holds on to the child, arms around the child's waist, fingers laced, and challenges the child to run to their parent, who is waiting with open arms. Child, of course, eventually breaks through the therapist's arms and makes it to the arms of their parent. This is best done when the child is reasonably comfortable with the therapist and is better for younger children. (T)

Silly Faces

One person makes a silly face at the other person, then the other person copies it. They take turns. This one can also be done in a group, passing the silly face around the group. (M E) (I)

Stand Up – back to back

Two people sit down on the floor back to back with knees bent and feet on the floor. They interlock their arms and then try to stand up. This is better for older children and will not work if the size between the people is too different. (T)

Stand Up – face to face

Two people sit down on the floor facing each other with feet touching toe to toe, and holding hands. They try to stand up together. Once they have done it successfully, they can be directed to do it again, maintaining eye contact throughout. This is better for older children and will not work if the size between the people is too different. (T E)

Thumb Wrestling

If you do not know how to play this, ask someone. Make sure it is all in fun and not too competitive. A good way to engage the child in non-threatening touch. Good for older children. (T) (I)

Touching Body Parts

One person calls out a body part, such as "elbow" and then everyone touches elbows. This is good both for dyads and larger groups. (T)

Touch Guess

One person closes their eyes, and the other person touches them as lightly as they can on their bare skin, and they see if the person can feel it. Then they trade. (T)

Tracing Shapes or Letters on the Back

One person traces with their finger a shape or letter on the other person's back, and that person has to guess the shape. Then they switch. I usually start out with a piece of paper with six shapes drawn on it (e.g., square, circle, triangle, cross, star, zig-zag) and have the participants pick from that. When they demonstrate proficiency with this, they then use numbers or capital letters. (T) (I)

Twinkle Twinkle (almost)

To the tune of Twinkle Twinkle Little Star, adults sing to child:

Twinkle twinkle little star
What a special child you are
With (say some things about the child), e.g., long long hair
And a bright sweet smile
Strong strong legs
And a smart smart brain

Twinkle, twinkle little star
What a special child you are.

The adults in the room can use whatever special qualities about the child that they like. They can touch the child as appropriate on each body part that they are talking about and can trade off coming up with positive attributes of the child. (T R)

Appendix B: Resources

There is a lot of information out there. Here are some of my favorites!

Attachment-Based Parenting

This book, written by myself, is designed to help parents help their children. Parents will not only learn about the underlying dynamics and motivations of attachment-injured children, but also how to create safety, build connection and, of course, how to reduce and address behavior.

Understanding Attachment Injuries in Children and Families: A Guide for Parents and Caregivers
by Catherine A. Young

These web pages were developed to share and support attachment-based parenting:

www.m-mat.org/attachment-based-parenting
www.m-mat.org/resources

Communication

My favorite book on parent/child communication is the classic:

How to Talk so Kids Will Listen and Listen so Kids Will Talk
by Adele Faber and Elaine Mazlish

This book has been around for a while, and there are now additional versions focused on very young children and teens.

Picture Books

These wonderful picture books highlight the enduring parent/child bond:

I'll Love You Forever
by Robert Munsch and Sheila McGraw

In My Heart
by Molly Bang

The Invisible String
by Patricia Karst and Joanne Lew-Vriethoff

I've Loved You Since Forever
by Hoda Kotb and Suzie Mason

No Matter What
by Debbie Gliori

The Runaway Bunny
by Margaret Wise Brown and Clement Hurd

Wherever You Are: My Love Will Find You
by Nancy Tillman

This delightful book highlights the specialness of each child:

On the Night You Were Born
by Nancy Tillman

Well-Respected Authors in the Field

The following are a few respected authors in the field of child trauma and attachment:

Bruce Perry, M.D., Ph.D
Daniel Siegel, M.D.
Bessel van der Kolk, M.D.

Appendix C:
Child Trauma and Attachment Terms

To capture the type of early trauma and neglect experienced by young children that may result in attachment difficulties, several terms have surfaced in the literature. Below are some commonly used terms related to attachment and early trauma.

Adverse Childhood Experiences (ACE) Study

The ACE (Adverse Childhood Experiences) study was conducted by Kaiser Permanente and the Center for Disease Control. Over 1700 individuals were recruited between 1995 and 1997, with subsequent long-term follow-up for health and other outcomes. Subjects completed questionnaires about Adverse Childhood Experiences, including child physical, sexual and emotional abuse; physical and emotional neglect; exposure to domestic violence; household substance abuse and mental illness; parental separation or divorce; and household member incarceration.

The study found that adverse childhood experiences (ACEs) are common. Perhaps not surprisingly, the number of ACEs an individual experienced was associated with increased negative outcomes in physical health (injury, chronic illness, infectious disease, maternal health); mental health (depression, anxiety, suicide, and PTSD); substance abuse and risky behavior; and poorer education, career, and income outcomes.

This study was notable because it was the largest study of its kind with tracking over time. It confirmed what many people perhaps already knew, i.e., that difficult early experiences can negatively affect many areas of one's life.

It is hoped that early intervention will help mitigate the impact of ACEs on an individual's life. That large-scale study is yet to be done!

Attachment Injury

An attachment injury is an impairment or injury in a child's attachment to their primary caregiver.

Attachment Styles

An attachment style is the way a child connects to their parent or primary caregiver. Four primary attachment styles have been identified in the literature related to young children. There is secure attachment, which one wants to strive for, and then three insecure attachment patterns: ambivalent, avoidant, and disorganized. All of the insecure patterns would indicate a child with an attachment injury. An insecure attachment style is the result of an attachment injury, just as a limp (a pattern of walking) can be the result of a leg injury.

These patterns were initially identified with toddlers, and so the definitions reference the behavior that occurs when these children are left in a "strange situation." The children were separated from their parent, exposed to a stranger, then reunited with their parent.

- **Ambivalent attachment (insecure)**: Child exhibits a very high level of distress when parent leaves. Upon parent's return, child may approach, then avoid or push away. Also appears anxious around stranger adults.

- **Avoidant attachment (insecure)**: Child avoids caregiver and displays no preference between caregiver and a complete stranger. This child does not seek out help or attention from adults.

- **Disorganized attachment (insecure)**: Child may exhibit a confused mix of behavior. May appear to freeze, be disoriented, wander, or have undirected or contradictory movement related to their caregiver.

- **Secure attachment**: Child shows distress when separated from parent and happiness when reunited. Child will consistently seek comfort, security, and attention from parent.

This is a fascinating area of study, and recently there has been discussion and work related to adult attachment styles. All of this, however, is beyond the scope of this book.

Complex Trauma and Relational Trauma

Complex trauma occurs when someone has experienced multiple traumatic events. It is differentiated from single incident trauma in that single incident trauma is a one-off situation, while complex trauma results from multiple events over time.

Trauma is relational when it is interpersonal in nature. That is, relational trauma is the result of one person traumatizing another, as in the case of child abuse or severe neglect or domestic violence. This is as opposed to other types of trauma, such as a car accident or natural disaster.

Many children who have experienced complex or relational trauma have injured attachment, particularly if a caregiver was instrumental or complicit in the trauma. Not surprisingly, complex trauma is generally harder to treat than single incident trauma. The individual's sense of self and worldview are more greatly affected by complex relational trauma than single incident trauma.

Developmental Trauma

Developmental trauma is complex/relational trauma at a young age that disrupts normal development. Children with attachment injuries have experienced developmental trauma, as the attachment injury interferes with the child's normal, healthy emotional development.

Developmental Trauma Disorder

Developmental Trauma Disorder was proposed as a new diagnosis for inclusion in the DSM-5 in an attempt to capture and provide a framework for treatment for those children who had early and repeated exposure to trauma (including emotional abuse and separation from primary caregivers). Criteria included emotional and physiological dysregulation, attention and behavioral difficulties, difficulties with self-esteem/self-image, and relational difficulties, when these symptoms lasted at least 6 months and caused significant distress or impairment in functioning.

As discussed previously, children with attachment injuries are not well captured in existing diagnoses. Developmental Trauma Disorder was proposed in order to better identify these children, and may have been a better fit; this diagnosis, however, did not make it into the DSM-5.

Dyadic Therapy

Dyadic therapy is therapy that works with the parent-child pair or dyad. A dyad is simply a pair of individuals. A dyadic relationship is the relationship between those two individuals.

Many therapy models addressing attachment, including M-MAT, are largely dyadic in that the healing of the child is presumed to occur primarily through the parent/child relationship. Once that relationship is addressed, a positive relationship template is created within the child, allowing them to function in other relationships.

Trauma-Informed

This term is used to denote approaches or programs that take trauma exposure into account. Trauma-informed care and trauma-informed practice are commonly used terms. Trauma-informed is a broad term that can be applied to many settings, including medical, academic, psychotherapy, and police services.

The idea is that when service providers have an understanding of trauma and the effects of trauma, they can respond in a more sensitive way to individuals with whom they interact. Agencies and organizations may develop specific "trauma-informed" practices to take trauma into account. This may be a teacher interacting with a student who has been exposed to domestic violence, a police officer interacting with a victim of sexual assault, or a medical provider working at a shelter for abused children.

About the Author

Catherine Young, LMFT, is an author, trainer, consultant, clinical supervisor, child and family therapist and parent. She has devoted over 25 years to helping children and families in settings as varied as children's day treatment, adoption and foster family agencies, child intensive mental health treatment, early childhood mental health, schools, juvenile probation, and private practice.

She is the creator of a new, practical therapy model for helping some of the most challenging children and their families: Multi-Modal Attachment Therapy (M-MAT). In her desire to share her ideas and bring healing to more children and families, she has authored two books:

On therapy:

M-MAT Multi-Modal Attachment Therapy: An Integrated Whole-Brain Approach to Attachment Injuries in Children and Families

On parenting:

Understanding Attachment Injuries in Children and How to Help: A Guide for Parents and Caregivers

CONTACT

Email: catherine@m-mat.org

Website: www.m-mat.org

Facebook Page:
www.facebook.com/MultiModalAttachmentTherapy